SLOW TRAVEL BRITAIN

Front cover photograph: Hollie Harmsworth
Back cover photograph: Beth Squire
This spread: Beth Squire

SLOW TRAVEL
BRITAIN

with
LODESTARS ANTHOLOGY

Compiled and written by
LIZ SCHAFFER

HOXTON MINI PRESS

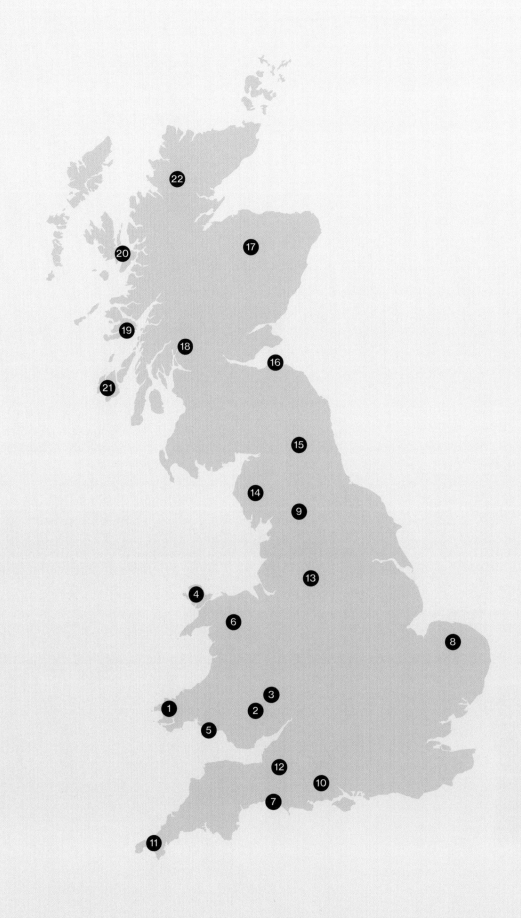

CONTENTS

Why go slow?

Slow travel is a tricky thing to define. If you take it right down to basics, it involves the act of moving slowly, perhaps opting to get around by trains rather than planes. But it can also mean embracing mindfulness (maybe with a spot of forest bathing) or seeking something that jolts you out of the ordinary, be that a stunning vista or an icy dip in the sea. At other times it entails doing nothing at all, merely finding a place that feels special and settling in for as long as itchy feet will allow.

My understanding of slow travel has evolved over the past decade. Before I founded *Lodestars Anthology* (a magazine that explores a single country every issue), I assumed slow travel was reserved for the daring. To join the fold, you had to own well-worn boots, crave high mountains and actively eschew creature comforts. But with each magazine I published, it became clear that slow travel was much simpler than this. While there might not be a fixed definition, it turns out that all you need when keen to move at an unhurried pace (be that physically or mentally) and be fully aware of the world around you is a sense of connection – to people, the past or even a landscape.

I've spent more than a year making this book, working alongside a team of wanderlust-fuelled photographers and, unsurprisingly, it's shifted my understanding of slow travel all over again. I was born and raised in Australia, but since 2011 England has been my adopted home, and Wales and Scotland my new neighbours. While living here, it's been fascinating to discover that we don't need to venture far, or for particularly long, to have a meaningful experience; awe can be found just one county over. Because when we're not jumping from far-flung destination to far-flung destination (an urge, I'll admit, that is hard to ignore), we are able to fully immerse ourselves in a location. We observe its rhythms, notice the little things and can start to feel as if we are part of the place we're exploring. Even the way we think might change – by submerging in a Munro-framed body of water or chatting to locals over coffee, we give creativity room to flourish and allow our minds to wander to some rather fascinating places.

But slow travel doesn't only encompass what we do on the road. It's also about being content with the experiences we've had. Rather than craving the next adventure, it sometimes pays to remember the sensations felt when standing beside a lore-steeped waterfall or ensconced in a centuries-old pub. As a travel writer, I'm always planning ahead. It's not that I forget to be in the moment, more that, when I start plotting future escapades, I don't always take the time to look back. Producing this book has allowed me to revisit the stories I wrote for the *Lodestars Anthology* England, Wales and Scotland magazines, returning (even if only in my mind) to some of the jaw-dropping hiking paths I've followed, boltholes I've swooned over and meals that changed my understanding of seasonality (and sparked my fondness for foraging). It's been astounding to realise how vivid those years-old exploits still seem; a fitting reminder that there are ways of holding onto the calm we feel when travelling, and they can be as simple as sitting down with a memory or a few fabulous photos.

While nature and connection are definite through-lines, these chapters also explore different ways of slowing down. Some will allow you to move in a more relaxed way by walking in wild weather beside Loch Lomond (p.190) or welcoming the restorative thrill of a cold water swim in

Eryri (p.64). Others are about spending time immersed in a community, perhaps getting to know Cornwall's creatives (p.118) or the whisky-makers of Islay (p.218). Others still will leave you enamoured with Pembrokeshire's hyper-local food scene (p.114), keen to fossil hunt along the Jurassic Coast (p.80), curious about the nuances of island life on Anglesey (p.46) and Mull (p.198) and aware of just how fascinating history can be – whether you're encountering it in the Yorkshire Dales (p.98), Skye (p.208) or along the North Coast 500, one of Britain's most phenomenal driving routes (p.228).

I hope this book inspires you to set off on an adventure, and to seek out connections and scenes that take your breath away. But most of all, I hope that you enjoy taking your time, whether you're on the road or delving into these pages.

Liz Schaffer
2024

About the Author

Liz Schaffer is the founder and creative director of *Lodestars Anthology*, an independent magazine that explores a single country in every issue, and is dedicated to food, nature, culture and life-changing experiences. An expert at living out of a suitcase, she is based between London and Sydney where she works as a writer, editor and photographer.

About the publisher

Hoxton Mini Press is a small indie publisher based in east London. We make books about London (and beyond) with a dedication to lovely, sustainable production and brilliant photography. When we started the company, people told us 'print was dead'; we wanted to prove them wrong. Books are no longer about information but objects in their own right: things to collect and own and inspire.

WALES

PEMBROKE-SHIRE

Explore the land through wild food

Photographs by Daisy Wingate-Saul

Pembrokeshire, tucked away in the far west of Wales, is a coastal haven with an abundance of sprawling beaches, artistic communities and wave-worn walking trails. When the sun shines (as it is wont to do here), you could almost believe you're on Antipodean shores; and if the weather gods aren't on your side, there's no shortage of snug pubs to abscond to. And while Pembrokeshire is the birthplace of coasteering and rich in sacred sites (all excellent reasons to visit), you travel here to eat.

There are restaurants worth building a trip around (Grove of Narberth's Fernery Restaurant springs to mind) and plenty of harbourside cafes dishing up flawless fish and chips, but it's the resurgence of foraging that makes things particularly special. Foraged elements elevate meals, tying you to the land and seasons and reintroducing the flavours and preservation techniques that our ancestors once knew so well.

I first tasted Pembrokeshire's bounty at The Little Retreat, a sustainability-focused glamping site in the estuary-framed hamlet of Lawrenny. Surrounded by bluebell-scattered woodland and watched over by the town's stone church, this site hosts an annual lifestyle festival, The Big Retreat,

Foraged elements elevate meals, tying you to the land and seasons and reintroducing the flavours and preservation techniques that our ancestors once knew so well

as well as chef Matt Flowers' Feast Pembrokeshire, an outdoor cooking experience which takes place in the property's restored walled garden (among other excellent settings). Matt, who also helms Tenby restaurant Tap & Tan with his wife Jade, cooks with fire, fusing this South American style (known for its deep, smoky flavours) with exceptional Pembrokeshire ingredients, such as foraged sea herbs and wild garlic. For him, cooking is a joy, a passion cemented during his first job as a teenager at the local pub, The Lawrenny Arms, just a 15-minute walk down the road. He'd start the day fishing on the estuary, sell his catch (often mackerel) back to the pub and then cook it during his shift. Then and now, he wants his flavour combinations to be recognisable, believing that the best meals have something familiar about them – be that potatoes just like the ones your grandmother used to make or a chicken that tastes as if it's been slow-cooked with love. Eating Matt's melt-in-your-mouth Pembrokeshire rump steak in the afternoon sun, with roses blooming around me, was a multi-sensory experience, offering a taste of the wealth of flavour found throughout the county.

An hour away, on Pembrokeshire's north coast, framed by forest, mudflats and the Preseli Hills, is Llys Meddyg hotel. Run by Ed and Lou Sykes, the restaurant team here are equally besotted with this rugged landscape, with Ed in particular keen to make foraging approachable for all. Treating his guided experiences like treasure hunts, he believes in bringing back a childhood sense of wonder. 'Foraging makes you think creatively,' he explains. 'What can you do with this blossom? Would this

work as a syrup or vinegar, could I pickle these seeds? Every ingredient is part of the party and has something to add.' Ed is also a fan of experimentation and collaboration (a recent project was with Still Wild distillery, which incorporates foraged Welsh botanicals like rowan and elderberries into its gins and vermouths) and his hotel's outdoor Secret Garden Restaurant includes foraged elements in almost every dish – many of which you collect while walking with him.

Foraging, especially as a first timer, can be daunting. There's so much to know, and missteps can have serious consequences – which is why it's best to venture out with an expert. Without having to worry about misidentification, you can indulge your curiosity, the world around you transforming into a surprisingly useful larder. With Ed, for example, I learned that stinging nettle can be made into hay-fever-alleviating tea; pennywort, with its pea-like flavour, is a great snack; the pectin in rowans makes it a brilliant setting agent; while primroses, with their soft flavour, are perfect for salads.

Dan Moar of Black Rock Outdoor Company and Forage Pembrokeshire is another expert who guides foragers throughout the county, with his experiences also focusing on bushcraft and rock pooling. A fount of all knowledge when it comes to a plant's homeopathic properties, he notes that nettle is protein-rich and has more iron, gram for gram, than spinach. Acorns, meanwhile, are a great coffee-substitute, and Dan thinks that

(right) Mwnt Beach, part of the Wales Coast Path

Ed believes in bringing back
a childhood sense of wonder

everyone should try making sticky hawthorn BBQ sauce (which comes with a subtle, tangy sweetness) or adding rosehip to their vodka for a tart, fruity twist. I left our walk with enough confidence to pluck the Jack by the Hedge I saw blooming that evening, the plant's garlicky, mustard-like taste making it a fab salad dressing addition.

Dan supplies (and runs foraging walks for) Annwn, a fine dining restaurant in Narberth that does phenomenal things with native Welsh ingredients. When I settled in for some culinary theatrics at Annwn the following night, I did my best to put the snippets of knowledge gathered with Ed and Dan to use, curious to see how preservation and cooking processes can change flavours – and just how many plant names I could remember. Inspired by Welsh history, Annwn's owner-chef Matt Powell has a nuanced understanding of seasonality and tradition. His multi-course (ever-changing) menu featured sea purslane picked that morning, preserved wild garlic, kelp broth (aged for three years, it was like eating the ocean) and gorse flower custard with birch vinegar that conjured memories of spring. While Matt is responsible for the gastronomic magic, you have to tip your hat to the land and all it produces.

Of course, there are other ways to connect with the wilds of Pembrokeshire, like absconding to fforest farm near Cardigan. Founded by Sian Tucker and James Lynch, this hideaway is part farm, part Japanese-inspired forest retreat, and is made up of a collection of bell tents, geodesic domes, hill and garden shacks crafted from cedarwood (more homely than their name implies) and a restored Georgian farmhouse. 'Every day we notice the light on the trees, through the clouds and on the sea, and the seasons passing, little by little,' Sian writes in her book *fforest: Being, Doing & Making in Nature*. 'We walk over the clifftops or pootle by boat across the sea to a secret beach and then set up a camp, collecting driftwood, making a fire and diving for spider crabs. We then cook over the flames and eat. We swim, we paddle and play games till sunset, then we head for home. This is as good as it gets. Cooking and eating, laughing and being outside with those you love is blissful for the body, for the heart and for the mind.'

And that's exactly what this wild and wonderful corner of Wales offers. Whether you're enjoying a foraged feast with those enamoured with the land and its bounty, or rambling through woodland, blackberries and samphire in hand, you feel connected and enthralled – linked to the people, the food and the environment. This is what slow travel is all about.

(left) Ed Sykes, co-owner of Llys Meddyg,
foraging for wild ingredients
(overleaf) A dish at Annwn restaurant; Jack by the
Hedge, found on a foraging walk with Dan Moar

DIRECTORY

The Pembrokeshire's Coast Path is accessible via public transport, making it easy to get around without a car. The route is part of the 870-mile-long Wales Coast Path, the first national trail anywhere in the world to wend along a country's entire coastline.

STAY

The Little Retreat

A luxury glamping site ensconced within the walled garden of a former castle, offering a range of wellness-boosting activities, from stargazing to yoga. Come for the annual Big Retreat festival in May.

littleretreats.co.uk
The Old Potting Shed, Kilgetty SA68 0PW

fforest farm

A nature-centric bolthole offering everything from bell tents to cabins framed by a kitchen garden – plus a sauna, plunge pool, woodland walks and Y Bwthyn (a tumbledown cottage that was rebuilt, stone by stone, into Wales' smallest pub). Nearby you'll also find Mwnt, a pristine beach on the Ceredigion coast overlooked by a 13th-century whitewashed church, and Cardigan, where the fforest team also run Pizzatipi, a pizza restaurant by the river.

coldatnight.co.uk/fforest-farm
Cwm Plysgog, Cardigan, Cilgerran SA43 2TB

Penally Abbey

This family-run country-retreat-meets-seaside-hideaway is dog-friendly and comes with the ruins of a 12th-century chapel in its sprawling gardens. It's also only a short drive from Tenby, a pastel-hued beachside town famed for its Georgian architecture and iconic lifeboat station. Each room in the hotel has a different shape and design, honouring the layout of the original house, with many featuring canopied beds, custom wallpapers and views across Carmarthen Bay. While seasonal sundowners in the art-filled terrace and drawing room are divine (the cocktails are finished with flowers and herbs from the garden), the jewel in the Penally Abbey crown is the 2 AA Rhosyn Restaurant and its multi-course, sustainable menu. Built around the seasons, foraged elements naturally feature in the dishes – including the wild garlic I spied blooming in Penally's woods during my stay.

penally-abbey.com
Penally, Tenby SA70 7PY

EAT

Llys Meddyg

Set within a Grade II-listed former Victorian coaching inn, this hotel is renowned for its foraging, with their finds spicing up meals served in the outdoor, flower-bedecked Secret Garden Restaurant and the indoor Dining Room, which features a wall-sized sorghum moss installation by artist Linda Minovca.

llysmeddyg.com
East St, Newport SA42 0SY

The Shed

Found along the Pembrokeshire Coast Path in the port town of Porthgain, this restaurant is much appreciated by hikers and serves some of the best fish and chips in the region, as well as a range of local seafood dishes.

theshedporthgain.co.uk
56 Llanrhian Rd, Porthgain, Haverfordwest SA62 5BN

Feast Pembrokeshire

Matt and Jade Flowers offer unique BBQ dining experiences and courses through their company Feast Pembrokeshire, cooking meals over the flames in various stunning locations. Available for private hire and catering, Matt also champions farmers and fishers from the region.

feastpembrokeshire.co.uk
The Mews, Upper Frog street, Tenby SA70 7JD

Annwn

An inventive fine-dining restaurant with a flair for showcasing superlative foraged ingredients and celebrating Wales' history. Its floors are cut slate, tables are carved from burr oak and handmade wooden cawl spoons double as wall art. Even the name Annwn is a nod to the past, referring to the Otherworld of Welsh mythology, a place of eternal youth where there's no shortage of food.

annwnrestaurant.co.uk
1 Market Square, Narberth SA67 7AU

DO

Hidden Routes Bike Tours

Explore Pembrokeshire's off-grid trails and hills via e-mountain bike with a guide from Hidden Routes Bike Tours. It's hard to wipe the smile from your face as you cycle through windswept, lamb-dotted fields after stopping by an Iron Age fort and raising a glass at the Dyffryn Arms.

hiddenroutes.co.uk
Llys Meddyg, Newport, Pembrokeshire SA42 0SY

The Pembrokeshire Coast Path

Covering 186 miles, this long-distance walking trail can be braved as one big adventure or in short, scenic sections. Highlights along the route include Abereiddi (the Blue Lagoon), a flooded slate quarry famed for its vibrant water and the ruins of an old wheelhouse, which is used as a diving ledge by the dauntless. There's also postcard-perfect Solva, swimmer-adored Broad Haven and Barafundle Bay and St Govan's Chapel. This tiny, 13th-century chapel is nestled within the cliffs and stands upon an earlier hermitage that was built as thanks by St Govan (said to have been a Knight of the Round Table), who sheltered here after being set upon by pirates.

Pembrokeshirecoast.wales/coast-path

Elvet Woolen Mill

Daniel Harris weaves custom Welsh blankets and cushions for fforest farm from Elvet Woolen Mill in the neighbouring county of Carmarthenshire. Bold and impassioned, he is restoring Elvet from its near-ruined state after its previous owner, at 93, insisted that he'd only sell it to someone who would continue running it as a weaving mill. Look out for Daniel's short courses, which he hosts when his custom milling jobs and restoration work allow.

instagram.com/londonclothco
Cynwyl Elfed, Carmarthen SA33 6TS

Abereiddi (the Blue Lagoon)

St Govan's Chapel

Llys Meddyg

Penally Abbey

Feast Pembrokeshire

fforest farm

Hidden Routes Bike Tours

Mwnt Beach

fforest farm

Llys Meddyg

fforest farm founder Sian and her son Jackson

BRECON BEACONS

Myth and folklore in Bannau Brycheiniog

Photographs by Beth Squire

Almost every time I head to Wales, I find myself in Bannau Brycheiniog (Brecon Beacons) National Park. Sometimes, I'll simply drive through, taking the slow route over the serpentine Black Mountain Pass. Other times, I'll find ways to draw the journey out, perhaps by stopping for a whisky tasting at Penderyn Distillery or going in search of Iron Age hillforts. Recently, I started to wonder exactly why this area keeps calling me back. Of course, there is much to love about Bannau Brycheiniog. It is both expansive and grand, a 520-square-mile natural wonderland stretching from Abergavenny to Llandeilo,

which contains brilliantly named icons like the Black Mountains and Fforest Fawr, a UNESCO Geopark. It has an abundance of hiking and biking routes and is an International Dark Sky Reserve (it was the first place in Wales to be awarded the accreditation back in 2012). But I've decided that what ultimately draws me back are the stories.

Talk to anyone about Bannau Brycheiniog's folklore and you'll learn that this is the domain of giants and fairies, and that almost every heather-filled valley or glittering lake comes with an age-old legend. Places steeped in lore have an aura, as if their mystique has been amassing over centuries,

Talk to anyone about Bannau Brycheiniog's folklore and you'll learn that this is the domain of giants and fairies

and as you start to delve deeper it's fun to let your imagination run wild. So, when I returned to the National Park for this book, I embraced the fantastic and visited sites where the myth was strong.

First up was Llyn y Fan Fach, tucked below the soaring, wave-like escarpments of Picws Du, the second highest peak of the Black Mountain Range. The route to this glacial lake is challenging, but wild swimming is an excellent reward – just be careful where you wade. If you believe the legend, a young man was grazing his cattle by Llyn y Fan Fach when a beautiful woman (they're always beautiful in these tales) emerged from its depths. He was instantly lovestruck, and when she told him that he'd become rich if they married, he keenly accepted, agreeing to the condition that if he struck her three times she'd return to the water. They lived happily on their farm with their growing brood for years and, as promised, his wealth grew – but so did his arrogance. Eventually he hit her, and on the third blow she strode back into Llyn y Fan Fach, taking the farm and animals with her (fair enough). On a happier note, the woman reappeared years later to tell her eldest son, Rhiwallon, that he and his family had a mission to heal the sick, leaving him with a bag of medicinal remedies. This is how the fabled 12th-century Physicians of Myddfai, pioneers of herbal medicine, came to be. As I waded into the still water myself, the sensation of

(left) Llyn y Fan Fach
(overleaf) Swimming in the River Wye, which flows through Hay-on-Wye in the northeast corner of Bannau Brycheiniog

being weightless after a long tramp uphill felt like its own kind of magic cure.

My second adventure took me to Waterfall Country in Bannau Brycheiniog's southwestern corner, a warren of rivers, gorges and caves. I'd come for the undulating Four Falls Trail, just one of the many walking routes that crisscross the area. The route delivers you, via a steep staircase, to Sgwd yr Eira, which translates as 'waterfall of the snow' – a nod to the fact that, when you're standing on the slippery, moss-covered rocks behind the falls, the spray looks almost like snow. The previous night, at The Felin Fach Griffin pub, a fellow patron told me that the waterfall is relatively close to Craig y Ddinas, a limestone outcrop reputed to be the resting place of King Arthur. The walk there isn't easy (or entirely safe), but perhaps that's for the best; Arthur is not someone you want to disturb.

The story goes that centuries ago, a stranger asked a Welsh drover crossing London Bridge where he'd found his staff, adding that, as a wizard, he could see it came from a place where treasure was buried. Excited by the promise of prosperity, the drover led him back to Craig y Ddinas and uprooted the tree from which he'd cut the staff. Underneath was a stone slab and steps leading to a corridor with a large bell hanging from the ceiling. Further in, he found a cavern filled with hundreds of slumbering warriors, and in their midst were 12 figures encircling a king. The wizard explained that this was King Arthur and his knights, who would sleep until the bell rang to signal the start of a mythic war.

Bannau Brycheiniog shows us how much there is out there to treasure and protect

Piles of gold, silver and precious stones lay around the warriors, and the drover was told that he could take whatever he liked, as long as he didn't ring the bell. He frequently plundered the hoard but, overly greedy one day (a plot twist we all saw coming), his laden sack knocked the bell and woke the warriors who violently threw him from the cavern. Destined to remain impoverished, he never found Arthur's tomb again.

For my final mythic outing, I returned to the mountains. Pen y Fan and Corn Du, two of the highest peaks in Wales, may look windswept and remote, but that doesn't stop them from luring close to a quarter of a million trampers every year. Renowned for their awesome views (you can see all the way to Somerset if you're lucky), both summits overlook the icy waters of Llyn Cwm Llwch. When the cloud is low and the light is soft, it's easy to believe that this lake contains an enchanted, invisible island – the domain of the *Tylwyth Teg* (fairy folk).

Centuries ago, a doorway was said to appear in a rock by the lake every May Day. Those brave enough to enter found themselves on a mystical garden island, where food and fantastic tales flowed. All the *Tylwyth Teg* asked in return for their hospitality was that guests take nothing home but memories. Yet we're beginning to notice a pattern in these yarns; greed reared its ugly head (as it so often does) and a man made off with a single flower. The moment he stepped back through the door he was robbed of reason. While the *Tylwyth Teg* continued to entertain their other oblivious guests, the door didn't reappear the following May Day, and hasn't been seen since.

Mulling over these stories while walking the landscape that inspired them, I understood their enduring relevance. With our world at a turning point and climate change weighing on everyone's minds, time in Bannau Brycheiniog shows us what is at stake, and how much there is out there to treasure and protect. These tales were, and remain, reminders to take only what we need (and ideally nothing at all), appreciate the good things and be sure to let sleeping kings lie.

(left) On the banks of Llyn y Fan Fawr. Bannau Brycheiniog was named an International Dark Sky Reserve in 2012

DIRECTORY

Unsurprisingly, summer is the most popular time to visit the National Park, when the weather is drier and the days are longer. But come in the colder months if you'd prefer a more solitary adventure – just remember your raincoat.

STAY

The Angel

Formerly a Georgian Coaching Inn, the Angel in Abergavenny has evolved into a swish and friendly boutique hotel. The classic interiors (elegant florals, dark wood and neutral hues) are adorned with a rotating collection of works from The Art Shop, a gallery and store dedicated to local practitioners found just up the road. As well as having some of the comfiest beds in Wales, you can abscond to the plush lounges with a cocktail, visit the in-house pub and bar and indulge at the Oak Room restaurant, where the seafood platter is especially mouthwatering – although you'll inevitably crave everything on the menu. It's lovely to see just how much locals adore this foodie destination; during my stay, every second table was claimed by patrons from Abergavenny.

angelabergavenny.com
15 Cross St, Abergavenny NP7 5EN

EAT

The Felin Fach Griffin

For a superlative Sunday roast (or elevated pub fare any day of the week) check out this cosy, dog-friendly, ochre-hued dining pub with rooms. Thanks to a menu that shifts with the seasons and a strong focus on sustainability, The Felin Fach Griffin has become a thriving community haunt.

eatdrinksleep.ltd.uk
Felinfach, Brecon LD3 0UB

The Walnut Tree

Found at the base of the Skirrid mountain at the eastern edge of Bannau Brycheiniog, the whitewashed, lantern-lined Walnut Tree is ideal for those who want to end a ramble with a Michelin-starred feast. The interiors are pared back, with vibrant art supplied by The Art Shop, yet what sets this venue apart is the warmth. Kick off proceedings with a cocktail in the garden, a flowering oasis backdropped by rolling Welsh hills.

thewalnuttreeinn.com
Llanddewi Skirrid, Abergavenny NP7 8AW

Have a picnic

If dining outdoors, gather supplies from The Angel Bakery (found across the road from the hotel), Brecon Chocolates and Chester's Wine Merchants, an Abergavenny wine bar and shop named after the owner's chilled-out hound. There's also Black Mountains Smokery, a sustainable outfit that smokes locally sourced meats, fish and cheeses and sells flour from Talgarth Mill, chutneys from Chepstow's The Preservation Society and much more besides.

DO

Tretower Court and Castle

Built by the Picards (daring Normans turned imposing Welsh lords) and extended and fortified during the War of the Roses by Sir Roger Vaughan, Tretower Court and Castle was abandoned in the 1700s and taken over by tenant farmers who converted stately rooms into pigsties and sheep pens. This may be part of the reason a restless spirit is said to haunt these now-restored halls. More than a few have spotted a woman in flowing white robes staring across the Usk Valley, believing her to be the ghost of Lady Margaret Vaughan waiting patiently for her husband, Sir Roger, to return. Unfortunately, Roger was beheaded at Chepstow in 1471, so alas the Lady in White waits in vain.

Powys, Tretower, Crickhowell NP8 1RF

Brecon & Beyond

Immerse yourself in the stories of Bannau Brycheiniog's largest town with this self-guided tour. The route, available through the Brecon Story website, takes in forgotten pleasure gardens (popular when William Turner came here to paint) and all that remains of the mills, reservoirs and breweries that boomed during the Industrial Age, as well as plenty of other Pagan, Norman and Celtic sites.

Other gorgeous visits include the Georgian town of Crickhowell, famed for its 18th-century bridge and found along the Beacons Way walking route; Talgarth, with its fabulous mountain bike trails and the remains of Bronllys Castle; Abergavenny, renewed for its annual Food Festival; and Hay-on-Wye, the world's first Book Town, which you can read more about in the following chapter.

breconstory.wales

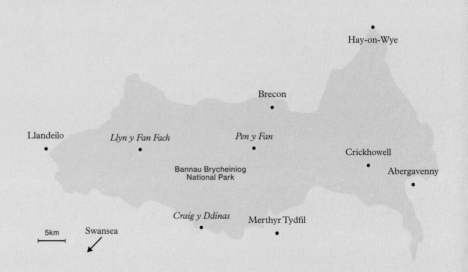

Bannau Brycheiniog National Park

The Angel Bakery

Crickhowell

The Walnut Tree garden

Tretower Court and Castle

The Oak Room restaurant at The Angel

HAY-ON-WYE

*Connection and conversation in a
world-famous literary town*

Photographs by Billie Charity

Bookseller extraordinaire Richard Booth crowned himself the King of Hay around the time he began transforming Hay-on-Wye into the world's first Book Town. Since then, it has become a hub for the literati, who flock to the annual Hay Festival every spring to celebrate books, art and ideas. But you don't travel to this picture-perfect border town for paperbacks and festivities alone. Since Booth opened his first bookstore in 1962, Hay has called to creatives of every ilk – from bakers and photographers to poets and lavender farmers – meaning that today you also come to Hay for imaginative, mind-opening conversations. And a good chat is always worth travelling for. After all, time spent with fascinating people (like time in picturesque places or with particularly excellent books) may just change the way we see the world.

My first Hay chat unfolded in one of the 30-odd bookshops in this densely literary town. Anne Brichto co-created the second-hand treasure-trove Addyman Books with her husband Derek in 1987 (the year Hay Festival was dreamt up), and their shop feels like something from another era. It's a rare gem where cosy nooks abound, pre-loved tomes grace every surface and you're encouraged

36

It's easy to overlook the impact of a passing conversation, those fleeting yet inspiring exchanges we have, especially while travelling slowly, with people we may never meet again

to take your time when searching for the perfect title. Anne believes that running a bookshop is all about creating magic. 'You're making a space where the book chooses you; you don't know what you will find. There's happenstance, serendipity, the weight of nostalgia when you see books from your childhood,' she explains. 'The whole point of a real-life bookshop is that you can just wander around and be surrounded by books. We have people who come in and just sit upstairs and read. That's so nice, to have other people around.'

Bookshops have always been places of wonder, but here that feeling is heightened. I was particularly smitten with the image Anne conjured of Hay in the decade before Addyman Books opened, when it was the stomping ground of hippies and farmers. As we chatted, she made me wish I'd seen this town in the somewhat ramshackle late '80s, a time when Anne and fellow booksellers would depart for boozy lunches, occasionally leaving customers accidentally locked in their stores.

There's something about travel that helps you open up. Removed from the familiar, curiosity ignites and strangers can quickly become friends. You're given an insight into the lives of others (all of which are as complex and nuanced as our own) and soon find that most people are happy to tell their tales, so long as we take the time to

listen. Hay, with its bohemian vibe and dedication to storytelling, encourages this interest. But I suspect that part of the reason conversation flows so easily here is because of the thriving sense of community. Everyone says hello, shares recommendations and supports others' work.

This rang true when I walked into Shepherd's Parlour, an ice-cream shop and cafe in the shadow of Hay Castle, and was greeted by an immense dried floral wreath crafted by local artist Layla Robinson. Clearly distracted by the piece while deciding between scoops of blackcurrant or honeycomb, I was told that Layla is always up for a chat – especially after one of her brilliant workshops. Inspired by the blooms of the Welsh borders, her ethereal sculptures are made using summer flowers from her garden, willow and birch foraged from the roadside in winter, bracken and berries plucked from the hills in autumn, and spring wildflowers. 'I want people to feel something very special when they look at my creations,' Layla says. 'Perhaps a subconscious connection with nature that makes them feel happy and alive.' Shepherd's isn't alone in promoting local talent. Almost every restaurant and store contains the work of Hay artisans and, if you're caught swooning over something, you'll most likely be offered an introduction (or at least a background story).

This is how I met Billie Charity, whose vibrant array of portraits (snapped around Hay over the years) hang alongside Layla's pieces at Shepherd's. Billie sees her camera as a way of connecting with

(left) Anne Brichto from Addyman Books
(overleaf) Locals chatting in Hay;
Nancy Durham from Farmers' Welsh Lavender

Bookshops have always been places of wonder,
but here that feeling is heightened

others. 'I remember a day in 2006 when I was in a pub with a friend,' she explains. 'I saw a man sitting in an old wooden chair, smoking and drinking a pint. To my friend's horror, I approached him and asked if I could take his photo. He was bemused but agreed. From that day I felt a whole new and exciting portraiture world opening up to me – strangers!

'I love the people I meet through photography and the interactions I have on the street,' she adds. 'When I stop people to ask if I can photograph them, they're often genuinely baffled, but always seem flattered. Many chat to me for a long time about their lives. I love that the camera gives me a way to meet people who I wouldn't otherwise have had the opportunity to meet.'

Wending my way through the heart of town, my bags getting heavier and heavier after picking up second-hand treasures in Green Ink Booksellers and Richard Booth's Bookshop, I stopped at the Farmers' Welsh Lavender shop, a cedar-clad, delicately scented haven beside the Hay clock tower. Journalist-turned-farmer Nancy Durham established a lavender farm with her late-husband, philosopher Bill Newton-Smith, atop a hill in nearby Builth Wells, and opened the store in town to sell products made with her distilled lavender oil, alongside wares from other creatives.

I asked why Nancy thinks conversation and connection feel so easy in Hay. 'There's so much going on – galleries, music, the cinema – and all the arty things that people are doing in and around Hay. And that draws people here,' she muses. 'You can have these deeper conversations, literary conversations, or conversations about art. They're part of the everyday. There's vibrant, cultural activity going on all the time. It's there in the background or you can delve in.'

This is a sentiment Layla shares. 'There really is a fabulous sense of community in Hay and the surrounding hills. Maybe this goes back through history, being a border town that's always had a lively and colourful past. Things feel possible in Hay, dreams feel achievable – and the people who live here really facilitate that. There is something about the fact that in some ways it has hardly changed over the years, but at the same time it's always evolving, welcoming in new people and situations.' Hay's allure may lie in the fact that – despite the books and creativity that define it – it really is just a small town, a place where you know your neighbours, champion all things independent and make the time to chat.

It's easy to overlook the impact of a passing conversation, those fleeting yet inspiring exchanges we have, especially while travelling slowly, with people we may never meet again. But there's a power to them; a chance to glimpse someone else's world or see our own in an entirely new light. So go to Hay, get lost in bookshops, smell the lavender and be sure to say hello. You never know where it will lead.

DIRECTORY

While you can visit Hay-on-Wye in any season, the town comes alive during the annual springtime Hay Festival. The main site (along with its pop-up bookshops) is free to enter, although you will need to buy advance tickets for individual events.

STAY

Llangoed Hall

You'll find this history-filled hotel just out of town, on the Welsh side of the border. Said to stand upon the site of the first Welsh Parliament, it was revamped by Clough Williams-Ellis (of Portmeirion fame) and saved from ruin in the 1980s by Sir Bernard Ashley (who filled it with the furnishings of his wife, Laura Ashley). The property is rounded off by a wildflower meadow, apple orchard and walled (chicken-housing) kitchen garden.

llangoedhall.co.uk
Llyswen, Brecon LD3 0YP

Cynefin Retreats

For a boutique stay with a twist, book one of these hand-crafted, self-catering cabins surrounded by seven acres of forest and farmland in the Wye Valley. These cleverly designed, contemporary spaces help you embrace the art of doing nothing, and come with wood-burning stoves, nature-inspired interiors, a woodland walking path and hot tubs perfect for stargazing. Waking up here to views of the Hereford Hills is decidedly good for the soul.

cynefinretreats.com
Cynefin Retreats c/o 3 Sheepcote Bungalows, Hereford HR3 5HU

EAT

The Old Electric Shop

Founded by ex-underwater photographer Hannah Burson, The Old Electric Shop serves scrumptious coffee and cake, but it's the interiors that win you over. The store is a treasure trove of vintage and contemporary finds – with its own bookshop, of course.

oldelectric.co.uk
Y Gelli Chambers, Broad St, Hay-on-Wye HR3 5DB

Kate's Bakery

If you're in town for Hay's Thursday or Saturday Market (the former has run for more than 700 years), stock up at Kate's stall, which sprang into existence more than a decade ago when Kate Brotherton Ratcliffe began baking bread at home and allowed the business to grow organically from there. Her canelés alone justify a visit.

instagram.com/katesbakeryhay
18 Lion St, Hay-on-Wye, Hereford HR3 5AB

Shepherd's Parlour

Do as the locals do and get your coffee and ice-cream from Shepherd's, where the art on the walls is sourced from Hay creatives and one scoop is never enough. Come festival time (and for most of summer) there's also an ice-cream van parked outside, while a second store has opened in Abergavenny, a town known for celebrating exceptional food.

shepherdsparlour.com
9 High Town, Hay-on-Wye, Hereford HR3 5AE

Chapters

Awarded a Michelin Green Star for their dedication to sustainability, Chapters is decorated with a forest of indoor plants, and grows many of their super-fresh, experimental ingredients in a garden eight miles from Hay. Visit for an array of sharing plates (I have nothing but praise for the braised red cabbage and fried Jerusalem artichokes) or a post book-buying tipple.

chaptershayonwye.co.uk
Lion St, Hay-on-Wye, Hereford HR3 5AA

DO

Hay Festival

Transforming the Town of Books since 1988, the springtime Hay Festival is all about sharing new ideas, inspiring audiences and encouraging change, which is achieved through brilliant programmes featuring writers, environmentalists, historians, actors and more than a few Nobel Prize winners. A second Welsh festival takes place in winter, while other events are held in Peru, Mexico, Spain and the USA.

hayfestival.com

Gospel Pass

For a superlative view, drive over Wales' highest paved road and gaze across a patchwork of undulating hills dotted with walking trails and curious ponies. Architecture and history buffs should pause at the wonky, yew-framed Capel-y-ffin, before continuing on to the regal ruins of the 12th-century Llanthony Priory. Surrounded by the Vale of Ewyas Hills, this is the perfect spot to partake in a G&T, served in the attached hotel's petite bar and imbibed as you rest against the remains of a medieval archway.

Farmers' Welsh Lavender

Founded by Nancy Durham and Bill Newton-Smith, Farmers' Welsh Lavender (the country's first lavender farm) is perched atop a hill just outside Builth Wells. While you can stock up on their treasures in Hay, visiting the farm allows you to swim in the pond, wander through a flowering garden, see the distillery at work and stay the night in Pantechnicon, a revamped truck-turned-two-person bolthole. Time your visit right, and you'll be able to catch one of their regular maker's markets too.

welshlavender.com/visit-our-shop-and-farm
Welsh Lavender Ltd, Cefnperfedd Uchaf, Maesmynis, Builth Wells, Powys, LD2 3HU

Addyman Books

There's no shortage of singular, conversation-inspiring bookshops in Hay, but Addyman Books is a personal favourite. Its owners Derek and Anne are also behind Murder and Mayhem (the place to go for detective fiction) and the slightly more daring The Addyman Annexe, a smaller sister bookshop.

hay-on-wyebooks.com
39 Lion St, Hay-on-Wye, Hereford HR3 5AA

Hay Festival

Cynefin Retreats

Farmers' Welsh Lavender

Llangoed Hall

Derek Addyman from Addyman Books

ANGLESEY

Embrace island time in North Wales

Photographs by Holly Farrier

It's surprisingly easy to fall in love with a place from afar. In fact, sometimes all we need to ignite that spark of wanderlust is a single image. The first photo I saw of Anglesey (Ynys Môn) was a drone shot taken by Holly Farrier – an abstract aerial scene featuring turquoise water, a pearl-white shore and just a hint of grassy hill. The light was golden, the sea calm and the photograph called to mind something far more exotic than we might imagine an island in North Wales to be. There were other images in her collection – a solitary lighthouse, a sandy expanse, pastel cottages – but after seeing that first shot, I couldn't get the idea of visiting Anglesey out of my head.

When I finally booked my trip, no longer able to ignore the siren's call of an island that's been the stomping ground of everyone from Romans to Vikings, it wasn't just the beauty I was travelling for. I was after a taste of quintessential island life, the chance to feel decidedly unhurried and let the weather and tides dictate my day. Island time is a strange phenomenon; an unrushed way of being where following natural rhythms, rather than a watch, has a way of removing worries and responsibilities from the equation. You'll get

*The mainland looms along parts of the
island's south coast, lying in wait just
across the narrow Menai Strait*

where you need to go… eventually, and will likely unearth a few treasures in the process.

Even driving on Anglesey (which spans 261 square miles) slows you down, the ever-changing views forcing you to stop, either to explore or simply drink in a vista. The mainland looms along parts of the island's south coast, lying in wait just across the narrow Menai Strait – the serrated outlines of Eryri National Park's peaks glowing blue in the early summer sun. Venturing north, past hidden beaches, churches built upon islands and neolithic burial cairns, the road delivers you to Parys, an abandoned mine where the land is a mix of ochre and gold, stained by the copper that has been extracted here since the Bronze Age.

Inspired by Holly's photos, I'd decided to make lighthouses the theme of my trip, using these stoic sites to bookend my days – the seven on and around Anglesey are architectural delights, after all. Beyond that, my plan was non-existent. One of the best things about embracing island time (and the laid-back attitude associated with it) is that you suddenly have room to improvise. Which is incredibly useful given that, when travelling, many of the most brilliant discoveries are often entirely unexpected. So, although I'd plotted a route that took in those aforementioned lighthouses, things were flexible. This meant that every time I found something beautiful, I was able to linger. In the end, I barely scratched Anglesey's surface, but what I saw was divine.

The photo that inspired my journey was taken at Penmon Point, so I made it – and the black and white Trwyn Du Lighthouse found there – my first port of call. Connected to a pebble beach by a causeway only visible at low tide (although walking across it at any time tends to involve getting wet), the lighthouse looks across to Ynys Seiriol (aka Puffin Island, a haven for these characterful sea birds). I'd come here for the stunning sunset, but it was the drive back to my homestay near Beaumaris that delivered the first unplanned gem – the stone remains of Penmon Priory. Found right beside the road, this 13th-century ruin evokes all the awe you'd expect from a crumbling sacred site, yet it was the priory's dark and curiously shaped dove-cote, built around 1600 and able to hold up to 1,000 nests, that proved most remarkable. Perhaps it was the time of day – the sun had dipped below the horizon, painting everything in a soft pink glow, and the lambs were bleating in hilarious harmony – but it felt as if I was already adjusting to the island's rhythms. There was nowhere to be and nothing to do, so I was free to take my time and embrace the dreamy scene before me. The road was so quiet that it was easy to forget this was the 21st century and parts of the Priory had been empty for hundreds of years. Even the dove-cote, which might have been ominous in the dusk, felt strangely peaceful.

A similar magic was at work on Llanddwyn Island, reached at low tide via a leisurely saunter along Newborough Beach. Crisscrossed by shell-strewn paths, this tiny island is home to a ruined stone chapel dedicated to St Dwynwen, patron saint of lovers, and crowned by Twr Mawr

Lighthouse, which looks out towards Eryri and the tropical Llyn Peninsula. Pausing in the sun by a row of whitewashed pilot cottages (in decades past their inhabitants guided ships carrying slate through the shockingly shallow Menai Strait), time once again became elastic, the veil between past and present gossamer-thin. Normally, surrounded by the noise and endless demands of our modern world, it's hard to feel transported; but here, with nothing to distract me but the glimmering sea, daydreaming came easily.

Just off Holyhead Island in Anglesey's north is South Stack Lighthouse, a spot coveted by bird watchers who vie politely for positions along the surrounding cliffs, seemingly unperturbed by the sheer drop to the water below. As I was visiting in June, the promise of communing with nesting puffins (from a respectful distance) more than justified the 400-step descent required to reach the lighthouse, which sits on a rocky promontory. I'm not sure how long I stood at its base, thoroughly entertained by these chatty creatures as they dived, swam and ran (rather inelegantly) along the water. But even this puffin circus (and my newly adopted, chilled-out approach to time) couldn't distract from the weather. The first summer heatwave had arrived with a vengeance, and when I eventually departed, the heat now biting, the walk back up to my car left me hot, sticky and in desperate need of a dip. So, journeying back across the island, I pulled off on a whim and plunged into the crystalline waters of Rhoscolyn, just one of the many beaches scattered along Anglesey's pristine coastline. Floating here between its rock pools and natural arches, with no schedule to keep and the sun determined to dally, island life was feeling pretty good.

(previous) The image of Penmon Point
that inspired the trip to Anglesey
(right) Trwyn Du Lighthouse at Penmon Point

DIRECTORY

Anglesey is connected to the mainland by the Menai Bridge, making it easy to reach by car or public transport – there's even a direct train to Holyhead from London.

STAY

Unique Homestays

Unique Homestays markets one-of-a-kind private holiday homes across the UK and Ireland. Out of their Wales collection, two can be found near Beaumaris: Saffron Tower, a 12th-century folly with a walled garden, sauna and pool; and Isla Windmill, a former flour mill where the '70s-inspired decor, spiral staircase and floor-to-ceiling windows pair perfectly with the epic coastal views.

uniquehomestays.com

EAT

The Bull

This dog-friendly village pub with rooms boasts more than 500 years of history, and a few nooks that have hardly changed since Charles Dickens visited in 1859. Its classic menu is built around fabulous Welsh ingredients from the land and sea, and it sits along the Beaumaris high street so you can visit after a spot of gallery-hopping around town.

inncollectiongroup.com/bulls-head-inn
Castle St, Beaumaris LL58 8AP

The White Eagle

Found at the top of the serpentine single-lane road that leads down to Rhoscolyn Beach, this chilled-out pub has a brilliant seafood menu and a terrace ripe for sun catching – a fitting addition given just how dazzling a sunny day on Anglesey can be.

white-eagle.co.uk
Rhoscolyn, Holyhead LL65 2NJ

Dylan's

The family-run Dylan's is an island staple. Their flagship, waterside Menai Bridge restaurant dishes up locally sourced seafood (like famed Menai mussels, which can sometimes contain pearls) and pizza, best paired with their own range of fabulous sauces and condiments (try the tangy pickled samphire). They also have restaurants in Gwynedd and Conwy.

dylansrestaurant.co.uk/restaurant
St George's Rd, Menai Bridge LL59 5EY

The Lobster Pot

Ideal for oyster and lobster devotees, this restaurant has been on the Anglesey foodie map since 1946. Here, it's all about seafood, and the friendly atmosphere is cemented by the fact that you'll likely be given winkles while you wait for your meal, assuming your visit aligns with the tides.

thelobsterpot.uk
Church Bay, Holyhead LL65 4EU

DO

Beaumaris Castle

Often referred to as 'the greatest castle never built', it's easy to let your imagination run wild here. Building began around 800 years ago under Edward I, but due to disappearing funds and distracting Scottish unrest, the castle was never completed – although this imperfection only makes it more remarkable.

Castle St, Beaumaris LL58 8AP

Halen Môn

Recover from lighthouse chasing with a seaweed bath in a reclaimed whisky barrel at Halen Môn salt factory. Seaweed is great for your body, packed with iodine, magnesium, zinc and omega, but the setting alone (surrounded by wildflowers and farmland, and with Eryri National Park across the water) is enough to calm a busy mind.

halenmon.com
Ty Halen, Brynsiencyn LL61 6TQ

Plas Newydd House and Gardens

Overlooking the Menai Straight and dating to the early 16th century, Plas Newydd (which means 'new house') is a National Trust-managed country home with lashings of military and artistic history. Its thriving gardens and grounds are easy to lose an afternoon in.

nationaltrust.org.uk/visit/wales/plas-newydd-house-and-garden
Llanfairpwllgwyngyll LL61 6DQ

Isla Windmill, Unique Homestays

Saffron Tower, Unique Homestays

Tŵr Mawr Lighthouse

Beaumaris Castle

The Bull

GOWER PENINSULA

Dip in and out of the Wales Coast Path

Photographs by Daniel Alford

In Wales nature dominates, the terrain shifting seamlessly from the sublime to the bucolic – which makes walking here an absolute joy. And while Eryri's peaks whisper to the intrepid and Anglesey feels surprisingly tropical, few places are more enticing to trampers than the Gower Peninsula, Britain's first Area of Outstanding Natural Beauty. Jutting out from southwest Wales into the British Channel, Gower is filled with secluded beaches, salt marshes, tidal islands and delicacies aplenty (such as cockles and seaweed), as well as a Michelin-starred restaurant and a distillery made for sun-seekers. Gower also lies on the Wales Coast Path, an 870-mile-long national trail that stretches from Chepstow in the country's south to Queensferry in the north. And although there's a lot to be said for tackling the entire route, one of the perks of hiking across Gower is that you can dip in and out of the Path, ending a ramble by the sea, stretched out on the dunes or nursing a pint in an atmospheric pub.

Despite the Wales Coast Path's popularity, I felt somewhat alone in Gower. I spotted walkers in the distance while hiking the coastal trail from Three Cliffs Bay to Oxwich, but for large stretches I only had the waves and gulls for company.

At Three Cliffs Bay, a sensational beach punctuated by limestone cliffs and tidal pools, I stopped to peruse my map beside the ancient walls of Pennard Castle. Gower is a lore-rich region, and it's fun to let yourself believe the improbable – like the myth that this 13th-century stronghold was built in a single night by a sorcerer, and later sunk into the sand when a king angered the *Tylwyth Teg* (fairy folk).

By the time I made it to Oxwich Bay (my adventure lengthened by a few detours over sand dunes), I'd fully embraced the perks of walking alone. Without the need to chat or entertain, you're free to move through the landscape at your own pace and focus solely on the scene before you. Sometimes all we need when hankering for clarity is space, nature and repetitive motion.

Solitude is a little harder to find at the 3-mile-long Rhossili Bay, home to Worm's Head, a tidal island that looks like a mythic creature rising from the deep. But that doesn't make it any less enchanting. Follow the headland walk for a better view of the island (sparing a thought for Welsh poet Dylan Thomas, who was caught out by the tides and stranded overnight as a child), before continuing to Gower's highest point, Rhossili Down. While you can spot North Devon on a clear day, the most picturesque things lie at your feet. The sweep of sand, the Helvetia shipwreck that was washed up here in 1887 and The Old Rectory, a stunning, semi-remote cottage built for a local priest in the 1800s so he could live halfway between his two parishes. Today, it's the bolthole of dreams, managed and rented out (to those who book far, far in advance) by the National Trust.

For something more daring there's Port Eynon in Gower's south (if you're on foot, you can visit as an extension of the Three Cliffs to Oxwich walk, or hike from Rhossili). Beyond the town's whitewashed houses and pebbly beach is a clifftop path that seems well-marked and leisurely… until it narrows and turns to lead you down to Culver

Hole. Should the wind stir up as you descend the steep trail to this near-hidden treasure, expect your heart to be very much in your mouth. But the experience is worth it. Standing before this immense, 60-foot-high cave, sealed behind a stone wall punctuated with curiously shaped windows, it's easy to imagine that it was once a smugglers' hideout – after all, Port Eynon's church and dunes were often used to hide contraband. It's far more likely, though, that Culver Hole was an ancient, wave-beaten pigeon coop.

Ultimately, what makes walking in Gower special is the diversity, with almost every route offering up something outstanding. Take, for example, my final saunter. After meandering through the wildflower-scattered pine forest of Whiteford Burrow in the region's north, I reached Loughor Estuary and the corroding remains of Whiteford Point Lighthouse. Built in 1865, it was decommissioned in 1926 and used for target practice by the RAF during the Second Word War. I only really understood the scale of this skeletal, cast-iron structure when I spied other beachgoers at its base, utterly dwarfed. Moody and beautiful, it bears the ravages of time and salt water well, standing as a reminder that even relics as stoic as this are destined to return to the waves.

Heading back across the sand of Whiteford Beach, my thoughts continued to unravel, the mental blocks and self-consciousness I trip over in everyday life carried away with the breeze. Swept up in the landscape, my ideas had time to run their convoluted course, and I ended up feeling so relaxed, so content with nothing but my footsteps and a view, that I started to wonder if I should just throw caution (and responsibilities) to the wind and spend a month or two attempting the entire Wales Coast Path – perhaps even continuing on to England's South West Coast Path and beyond. Walking is always wonderful, a way to dust off the everyday and revel in the world around us. But walking in Gower is something else entirely.

(previous) Sunset over Three Cliffs Bay
(overleaf) Hunts Bay and Rhossili Beach

DIRECTORY

*It takes four to seven days to walk the entire 65-mile route around the Gower Peninsula,
but there are plenty of shorter hikes in the region: try Rhossili to Port Eynon (7.5 miles)
for a wildlife-rich landscape, or Oxwich to Pennard Cliffs (5.25 miles) for flat, sandy
stretches. Further walks are listed on the Visit Wales website.*

STAY

The King Arthur Hotel

This historic, family-run country inn is so
laid-back that even sheep are welcome and are
often seen grazing in the beer garden. The
King Arthur Hotel is also a short walk from
Arthur's Stone (Maen Ceti), a Neolithic hilltop
burial chamber with views across ferns and
paddocks to Whiteford Burrows in one direction
and the Bristol Chanel in the other.

kingarthurhotel.co.uk
Higher Green, Reynoldston, Gower SA3 IAD

The Old Rectory

This four-bedroom cottage (a former priest's
house dating from the 1800s) is made for those
looking to get away from it all. Almost entirely
alone on Rhossili Beach, sheep are your only
neighbours, and all you can hear come night
are the waves.

nationaltrust.org.uk/holidays/wales/rhossili-old-rectory
Rhossili, West Gower, Swansea SA3 IPL

EAT

Gower Seafood Hut

Parked along the Mumbles waterfront and
backdropped by candy-coloured houses, this
is the creation of Sarah Kitt, granddaughter of
a Swansea trawler-man, and Chris Price, who
spent his teenage years on fishing boats. Their
dedication to fruits de mer shines through
in their fritto misto – sardines, whitebait and
squid flavoured with samphire, and particularly
scrumptious with spoonfuls of their garlic mayo.

instagram.com/gowerseafoodhut
Southend Gardens, Promenade Terrace, Mumbles,
*   Swansea SA3 4DS*

Beach House Restaurant

Embrace your inner gourmand at the Michelin-
starred jewel in Gower's culinary crown. While
chef Hywel Griffiths showcases produce from
across Wales, much hails from the peninsula
itself. Gower Salt Marsh Lamb, Swlwyn's
Seafoods and Oxwich Bay Lobster and
Bass are just some of the exceptional local
suppliers used.

beachhouseoxwich.co.uk
Oxwich Beach, Swansea SA3 ILS

The Pubs

Post-hike recoveries should always involve
a long lunch at an excellent pub, and two of
Gower's best are Port Eynon's family-run, pet-
friendly Ship Inn, which is ideal for those fond
of seafaring decor, and Llanmadoc's flower-
bedecked Britannia Inn, which pairs classic
pub fare (their Sunday roasts are revered)
with a sweeping salt mash view.

shipinngower.co.uk | 10 Strand, Port Eynon,
*   Swansea SA3 INN*
britanniagower.com | Llanmadoc, Swansea SA3 IDB

DO

Castle Ruins

Wales has more castles per square mile than
any other European nation, and you can cross
a few regal ruins off your list in Gower. Pay
your respects to the 700-year-old Weobley
Castle, high above the Llanrhidian marshes,
or the 12th-century Anglo-Norman Oyster-
mouth Castle in Mumbles. And then there's
Pennard Castle, a ruin by Three Cliffs Bay
that's steeped in lore and thought to have a
resident banshee.

The Gower Gin Company

Get into the holiday spirit (pardon the pun)
with Siân and Andrew Brooks' award-winning
distillery. The Gower Gin Company is inspired
by the region, with their original GŴYR gin
capturing the coast through foraged green and
bronze fennel, while Rhossili comes with hints
of sea blackthorns and gorse. You can sample
the full range in their gin garden, a welcome
haven after a day braving the Coast Path.

thegowergincompany.wales
Highfield, Port Eynon, Swansea SA3 INL

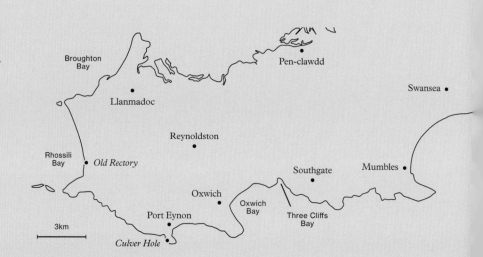

Beach House Restaurant

Beach House Restaurant

The King Arthur Hotel

Rhossili Beach and The Old Rectory

SNOWDONIA

Cold water swimming beneath Eryri's mountains

Photographs by Hollie Harmsworth

Rain was approaching and the air was thick with summer humidity; conditions that meant I had Llyn Tegid (on the western edge of Eryri National Park, formerly Snowdonia) all to myself. As I stepped gingerly over pebbles, the lake clear and still despite the grey sky, I noticed that I was already breathing slower. Yet when the water reached my shoulders, I couldn't help but gasp. In that moment, all I thought about was the biting temperature and the prickling sensation up and down my legs – a shock response that was replaced almost immediately by a sense of release. Around me, the forest-cloaked hills were low, but

rather than being entertained by this melange of green, I looked up at the clouds and remembered just how much I adore the water.

I grew up in Australia, so my childhood swimming memories are a little different. I recall diving beneath the waves on scorching summer days (when being underwater felt like the only reprieve from the heat) and returning home sun-kissed and elated, dusted in salt and sand. As I got older, I was drawn to calmer settings, getting lost in the soothing sameness of gliding up and down a pool lane, savouring the clarity that comes with something so repetitive. Swimming became more

Covering 823 square miles and home to nine mountain ranges and 74 miles of coastline, Eryri National Park is a maze of walks and waterways

bracing when I moved to the UK. But even if the activity now requires a dash of courage (or, failing that, a wetsuit), the serenity remains. Floating in mountain lakes or the Hampstead Ponds, my body still unwinds and my thoughts unknot, the rest of the world drifting away as I get swept up in my watery realm.

Whatever the hemisphere, I know swimming relaxes me, but I've always wanted to better understand the mechanics that make cold water swimming so wondrous and felt that the best place to do this was somewhere wild. So, I headed north to Wales' largest national park, a place once dominated by mines. It is now a jumble of forests and staggering peaks, which make the landscape so lush and expansive that it doesn't seem to be entirely of this world. Covering 823 square miles and home to nine mountain ranges and 74 miles of coastline, Eryri National Park is a maze of walks and waterways. Those drawn to its cool, watery depths can float in glens where the spirits feel close, expanses like Llyn Cwm Bychan (a lake immortalised in Roger Deacon's homage to British wild swimming, *Waterlog*) and Llyn Llydaw, believed to be Excalibur's final resting place (although Llyn Ogwen shares this mythic claim to fame).

Exhilarating as it may be, wild swimming can be treacherous for the uninitiated, and the safest way to submerge is with a local guide. Enter

Sheena Corry, who runs The Forge with her husband Jamie, a bushcraft specialist besotted with trees. Found just east of Eryri National Park, The Forge is an off-grid glamping haven replete with bell tents, a cacophonous dawn chorus and a hillfort blanketed in harebells, yarrow and yellow rattle. It's a setting where time loses meaning, and an entire evening can be spent by the fire, taking a strange delight in watching a dormouse emerge from its burrow and an owl return to roost among the rowan roots.

Guests stay at The Forge during Sheena's wild swimming retreats. Although she's always swum in the sea – a hobby picked up during her North Wales childhood – she didn't start wild swimming properly until the pandemic, when she promised herself that she'd paddle in the River Dee once a week until winter took hold. But the calm that came with swimming, the chance to reset, made it impossible to stop, even on the frostiest of mornings. 'From a mental health perspective, I found that on the days I went swimming, I was able to deal with the anxiety that came with navigating a small business through the pandemic so much better,' Sheena explains. 'The problems hadn't gone away, but the way I was reacting to them was quite different.'

Keen to understand this shift in her outlook, Sheena started doing some research and was blown away by the sheer number of natural chemicals released when a body is exposed to cold water. 'You get 250 per cent more dopamine, which lasts for at least two hours – and sometimes for the rest

(left) Llyn Du'r Arddu, in the mountains, is a quiet spot to swim
(overleaf) Walking trails and fishing lakes in the Migneint

In that moment, all I thought about was the biting temperature and the prickling sensation up and down my legs

of the day,' she explains. 'And you get a hit of serotonin and a big rush of endorphins while you're in the water because your body goes into a managed shock response. So you have this amazing high when you're swimming, but also this lovely, calm, gentle feeling for the rest of the day.'

Sheena constantly adds new swimming spots to her repertoire, orientating family walks towards potential pools and waterfalls, although it's not just her collection of lesser-known sites that entices retreat participants. 'After our first weekend, it was clear it was about so much more than wild swimming,' says Sheena. 'It's about a community of people coming together. Being in the water and staying off-grid creates a real openness. Everyone is willing to share their stories and be really honest about why they are there.'

Wild swimming experiences are subjective. While you may share the water with others, what you take from it can be vastly different, shaped by the smallest things – like your reaction to the air temperature, how much sleep you've had or your mood on the day. But the one common factor is the natural high. This chance to give yourself over to the elements, to try something daring with a group of strangers, almost always relaxes and invigorates you. It's impossible not to feel exhilarated; so it's little wonder that once you start cold water swimming, you'll inevitably crave more.

Thankfully, in Eryri there's no shortage of places to submerge. 'We're totally blessed here,' agrees Sheena. 'We've got the River Dee, which starts in the National Park and travels all the way to Chester; there's apparently a family of otters for every mile of river. And we've got Wales' largest natural lake, Llyn Tegid, with a species of fish called the gwyniad that was left behind at the end of the last Ice Age, and can only be found in the deepest parts of the water here. And there are so many waterfalls – some that people know about, and some of which are hidden. That's my absolute passion: seeking out those secret spots.'

I spent my final Eryri day somewhere not-so-secret: the Fairy Glen, a short drive from the hiker-adored stone town of Betws-y-Coed. A storm had raged the previous night, illuminating my Forge bell tent with brilliant flashes of neon, and the Fairy Glen was now too treacherous for swimming, its normally still pools replaced by dark, fast-flowing water. But as I meandered along the forest path beside the rapids, I still felt soothed. Pine trees scented the air, sunlight twinkled and all I could hear was the rush below. Few things are as powerful as swimming somewhere wild. But on that day, simply being near the water was enough, its power and beauty tiding me over until the next time I could submerge.

(overleaf) Looking out over Llynnau Mymbyr,
two lakes in the Dyffryn Mymbyr valley

DIRECTORY

*If you're new to wild swimming, it's always best to venture
out with a guide – and if you're looking for a more
substantial experience, join a retreat at The Forge.*

STAY

The Forge
Watched over by an Iron Age hillfort, this off-grid glamping site specialises in wild swimming and wellness retreats that are designed to help guests get back to nature. You can stay in a bell tent or the gypsy caravan (all include private kitchens, terraces and outdoor fireplaces), and there's also a book-filled communal area and yoga space. Breakfast and BBQ hampers can be arranged, or simply stock up en route with supplies from the organic Rhug Estate Farm Shop.
theforgecorwen.co.uk
Cae einion, Corwen LL21 9BY

Bodysgallen Hall
Beginning life as a medieval watchtower and now one of the National Trust's Historic House Hotels, the pink-sandstone Bodysgallen Hall sits within 200 acres of parkland and gardens, a bewitching assortment of orchards, wildflowers, woodlands and lily-dusted ponds. Comprising suites, lavish rooms, converted cottages (found near the spa) and a 3AA Rosette restaurant (with views across to Conwy Castle), it oozes old-world luxury.
bodysgallen.com
*The Royal Welsh Way, Bodysgallen Ln,
  Llandudno LL30 1RS*

Portmeirion
Purpose-built over six decades by self-taught architect Sir Clough Williams-Ellis, Portmeirion is an eccentric, pastel-hued fantasy; a village-meets-holiday-resort borrowing elements from almost every architectural style. Known as a 'home for fallen buildings', Clough accepted features from properties facing collapse after the Second World War – from facades and fireplaces to the Bristol bathhouse's colonnade – and incorporated architectural tricks to play with perspective and create a strange sense of cohesion. Ultimately, he wanted everything to honour the natural setting – after all, it was the cliffs by the Dwyryd Estuary that made him believe this was the perfect spot to build his dream village. Striking and bonkers, it feels as if Portmeirion has been watching over the tides for centuries.
portmeirion.wales

EAT

Ynyshir
Found just south of the National Park in a country house once owned by Queen Victoria, this restaurant with rooms is a two Michelin-starred culinary wonderland. Created and run by chef patron Gareth Ward, the music is loud (there are disco balls and resident DJs). Foodie rules are regularly broken and the tasting menu stars local foraged finds – the result is a meal worth crossing the country for.
ynyshir.co.uk
*Ynyshir Restaurant and Rooms, Eglwys Fach,
  Machynlleth SY20 8TA*

Pen-Y-Gwryd Hotel
Sir Edmund Hillary and Tenzing Norway came to Eryri to train before summiting Everest, and the ivy-clad Pen-Y-Gwryd Hotel is where they chose to stay. Stop by for a drink and to soak up the mountaineering history.
pyg.co.uk
Nant Gwynant, Caernarfon LL55 4NT

Penmaenuchaf
Enveloped by 19th-century terrace gardens, this stone-fronted Victorian mason house (turned hotel) boasts a phenomenal restaurant. The North Wales-inspired menu is the work of chef Tom Hine, who honed his skills working for British culinary icon Michael Caines, and led Coast restaurant in Saundersfoot, a famed Pembrokeshire institution.
penmaenuchaf.co.uk
Penmaenpool, Dolgellau LL40 1YB

Coffee & Cake
Refuelling after a wild swim is essential, so if you've got coffee and cake on your mind head to Tu Hwnt I'r Bont (which translates to Beyond the Bridge), a tearoom found in a 15th-century, ivy-cloaked building beside the River Conwy. Just beyond the hiking and swimming hub of Betws-y-Coed is Ty Hyll (The Ugly House), where *bara brith* and other baked treats are served in a charming cottage surrounded by volunteer-run gardens and beehives.
*tuhwntirbont.co.uk | Ty Hwnt I'R Bont Cafe, Llanrwst
  LL26 0PL*
Ty Hyll: Betws Rd, Capel Curig, Betws-y-Coed LL24 0DS

DO

Dyfi Distillery
Founded by brothers Danny and Pete Cameron, who brought with them knowledge of foraging and environmental science (Pete) and the world of wine and spirits (Danny), the sustainability-driven Dyfi Distillery – nestled in the Dyfi Valley, at the southern end of Eryri National Park – specialises in gin that tastes of the place it's made. Classic base ingredients of citrus and juniper are paired with hyper-local botanicals such as bog myrtle, Scots pine and heather, harvested from the UNESCO-designated Dyfi biosphere.
dyfidistillery.com
Unit 5, Craft Centre, Corris, Machynlleth SY20 9RF

Corris Mine Explorers
Beside the distillery, an abandoned slate mine made up of 84 hand-hewn chambers and miles of underground tunnels is managed by the team at Dyfi. Tours guided by Corris Mine Explorers – mining historians and archaeologists (who prefer the title 'geeks') – help you see this subterranean world as miners once did.
corrismineexplorers.co.uk
Corris Craft Centre, A487, Corris, Machynlleth SY20 9RF

Vintage Trains
Porthmadog is a train enthusiast's dream, a site where two meticulously restored historic railways meet. Originally used for hauling slate, the Ffestiniog Railway was transformed into a tourist railway in 1982, while the Welsh Highland Railway (a passenger service to Caernarfon, established in 1922) reopened in 2011 after its lines, ignominiously lifted during the Second World War, were re-laid. These astonishing trains trundle, climb and spiral through Eryri's intoxicating landscape of cloud drift and ever-changing colour, and it's impossible to not be awed by the dedication that brought these routes to life once more.
festrail.co.uk

Wild Swimming
There are countess places to swim in Eryri, from the expansive Llyn Tegid and the icy Llyn Cau (requiring a walk to reach) to Llyn Padarn, which comes with views of Yr Wyddfa

Bodysgallen Hall

The Forge

Corris Mine Explorers

Penmaenuchaf

Ynyshir

Portmeirion

Bodysgallen Hall

Portmeirion

Ynyshir

Llynnau Mymbyr

Penmaenuchaf

Llyn Bychan

Dyfi Distillery

Penmaenuchaf

ENGLAND

JURASSIC COAST

Unearth England's prehistoric past

Photographs by Beth Squire

Looking up at the statue of Mary Anning on the Lyme Regis promenade, chisel in her hand and hound at her heel, I can feel my fossil-fever take hold. With the sea spray stirring, it's easy to picture blustery days in the early 1800s when this heroine of palaeontology spent hours scouring the nearby cliffs for prehistoric creatures – beasts whose existence was doubted by many at the time.

Mary's numerous finds (including the skeleton of a 17-foot-long *Ichthyosaur* that she unearthed as a 12-year-old) challenged dominant ideas about the history of life on earth (by providing compelling evidence of evolution) and put what we now

know as the Jurassic Coast on the geological map. Stretching for 95 miles from Exmouth in Devon to Old Harry Rocks in Dorset, this unique coastline captures an astonishing 185 million years of history. Having once been a desert, ocean and marsh, it is the only place on Earth where rocks from the Triassic, Jurassic and Cretaceous Periods are found in one place. It's been declared a UNESCO World Heritage Site, an Area of Outstanding Natural Beauty and a Site of Special Scientific Interest – and is where you venture, as I did, when you want to feel dwarfed by the staggering passage of time.

Having once been a desert, ocean and marsh, it is the only place on Earth where rocks from the Triassic, Jurassic and Cretaceous Periods are found in one place

Today, the Jurassic Coast is still a fossil-lover's nirvana, with erosion (caused by frequent storms and the battering of waves) continually revealing the fantastic remains of long-extinct organisms. Ammonites – shelled cephalopods that last swam in the seas around 66 million years ago – are the most prolific, but even these can be tricky to uncover at first. Seek out a guide at the Lyme Regis Museum or Charmouth Heritage Coast Centre for a better chance of discovering something exciting. Combing the beach for treasure may feel a little illicit, but fossil hunting is encouraged along the Jurassic Coast, given that the alternative is having potential finds washed away into the deep.

History is etched into the landscape here, from the coiled marvels hidden along its beaches to the dramatic arches, pinnacles and stack rock carved by aeons of wild seas. Undulating farmland tumbles toward the coastal fringes, where the water is coloured a striking turquoise by the chalky sand. Add postcard-perfect villages, beaches that stretch for miles and pearl-white cliffs, and you've got a landscape that is equal parts dramatic and sublime. The Jurassic Coast took millions of years to form and is constantly changing, remains from the past tumbling from the cliffs with every bout of brutal weather. In such a setting, you want to take things slowly, and give the beauty the time it demands.

(previous) Old Harry Rocks
(left) Man O' War Beach, found behind Durdle Door, a natural limestone arch

Lyme Regis, Mary Anning's hometown, is a hive of laneways, artist studios, museums and gardens (once roamed by Jane Austen). Things feel particularly peaceful in the early morning, when the empty streets and soft dawn light make you wonder if you've travelled back in time. With a row of pastel beach huts behind me, I sat on the pebbled beach just after sunrise, absent-mindedly twirling rounded stones in my hand while watching swimmers approach the waves. Each spent more time mulling over the conditions than they did actually submerged, although the conversations and trepidation were clearly part of the fun.

At the eastern edge of the Jurassic Coast stand Old Harry Rocks, striking monoliths that rise from Studland Bay like chalky, glowing juggernauts. These natural sculptures have taken shape over the past 100 million years, formed from a band of chalk that stretches all the way to the Isle of Wight, about 15 miles away. If the sky is clear and the light just right, you might be able to spy The Needles, chalk stacks perched at the tip of the Isle that were thought to have once been connected to Old Harry by a chalk wall eroded over thousands of years. Time has been equally cruel to Old Harry's Wife, a single stack beside Old Harry that fell into the sea in the late 1800s, leaving just a stump in her place – a striking reminder that, in the grand scale of time, we're simply passing through.

If you want a guaranteed fossil encounter, then drive east to Kimmeridge Bay, a site adored by smugglers in the 17th and 18th century thanks to its natural rock ledge and shallow waters. The village of Kimmeridge is now home to The Etches Collection Museum of Jurassic Marine Life, which contains around 2,000-odd specimens, all found by Dr Steve Etches MBE, a plumber-turned-palaeontologist who established the museum in 2016. Moving through the space, I was awed by the time and dedication this fossil hunting would have demanded, and it was fun to imagine the thrill Steve must have felt with each new discovery – like the one he recently made with his friend Phil Jacobs. Phil initially found the snout of a *Plesiosaur* (a terrifying marine reptile) on a nearby beach in mid-2022, after it fell from the cliff. Steve and Phil then located the rest of the 6.5-foot-long, teeth-filled skull, which Steve extracted – a complicated and dangerous process given the cliff's fondness for crumbling. This significant discovery, and Steve's desire to find the rest of the beast, proves that, all these years later, Mary Anning wasn't alone in her passion for unearthing the Jurassic Coast's treasures. Generations have been inspired by her work – called to this coastline for the monsters it might contain as much as the astounding beauty – and that's a remarkable legacy to leave behind.

DIRECTORY

*Fossil hunting is a year-round pursuit, but you're most likely to find
something in winter or early spring, when storms erode the coastline and
crumbling cliffs deposit fossils onto the beach.*

STAY

Glebe House

Overlooking the Coly Valley, this six-bedroom
retreat (with an additional cabin), is known as
a restaurant with rooms – or rooms with a chef.
Dinner is the star attraction, whipped up by
Glebe House co-owner Hugo Guest, who grew
up here and is passionate about local produce
and the Slow Food ethos. Everything tastes
as if it's just been plucked from the kitchen
garden, pulled moments ago from the oven or
cured in his purpose-built ageing room. Much
of the decor is the work of his wife and fellow
owner Olive, a third-generation artist who
paints brilliantly hued abstract landscapes.
The eclectic array of vibrant art is balanced by
the home's Georgian bones and chic bohemian
vibe. There's a glass-encased entrance draped
in vines and canvases, hand-painted lamp-
shade inspired by the Bloomsbury set and
newly upholstered vintage furniture. Few
places feel quite so creative – or come with
such bucolic views.

glebehousedevon.co.uk
Southleigh, Colyton EX24 6SD

Dorset House

This boutique and welcoming Lyme Regis
B&B is devoted to sustainability and adored
for its multi-course breakfast. Furnishings are
modern and comfortable but there are nods
to the Georgians (who came to Lyme Regis to
take the sea air) in the fireplaces, chandeliers
and antique waxed floorboards. Throughout
the house are hand-pressed seaweed prints
from Molesworth and Bird, a creative duo
whose store is part of the town's Old Mill
Artistic Hub – just one of the attractions that
appear on owner Lyn's perfectly curated,
hand-drawn welcome map.

dorsethouselyme.com
Pound Rd, Lyme Regis DT7 3HX

EAT

The Pig on the Beach

Part hunting lodge and part beach cottage, The
Pig on the Beach looks like a turreted ginger-
bread house, and is made for long lunches,
with all the restaurant's ingredients sourced
from within a 25-mile radius. In keeping with
the garden-to-plate ethos, the team grows as
much as possible in the on-site kitchen garden,
and many of the accompanying wines are
hyper-local, the sparkling rosé from Dorset's
Langham Wine Estate a standout. After lunch,
lounge by the garden bar, book a spa treatment
or meander over chalky grassland to Old Harry
Rocks and while away the rest of the afternoon
watching kayakers navigate these Dorset icons.

thepighotel.com
Manor House, Manor Rd, Studland, Swanage BH19 3AU

Lilac Restaurant & Wine Bar

Lilac proves that wine tastes better when imbibed
inside a 400-year-old cellar. Their small plates
menu features organic ingredients, the sustainability efforts are commendable and the cocktails
are daring. It's little wonder this has been praised
as one of the best date night spots in Dorset.

lilacwine.co.uk
57-58 Broad Street, Lyme Regis, DT7 3QF

Catch at the Old Fish Market

Found along the Weymouth waterfront, the
Catch's ever-changing menu is designed to
reflect the diversity of the seasons, and is
ultimately shaped by what fishing boats bring
back that morning, so expect something truly
innovative.

catchattheoldfishmarket.com
1 Custom House Quay, Weymouth DT4 8BE

DO

Corfe Castle

A site of murder, siege and romance, Corfe
Castle (a striking hilltop ruin managed by the
National Trust) is one of England's earliest
stone castles. Walk along its base and you'll
pass massive chunks of wall that are now
embedded in the earth where they fell during
the English Civil War. Corfe is a stop on the
volunteer-run Swanage Railway, which allows
you to admire the Purbeck landscape (an Area
of Outstanding Natural Beauty) aboard vintage
steam and diesel trains.

nationaltrust.org.uk/visit/dorset/corfe-castle
The Square, Corfe Castle, Wareham BH20 5EZ

Durdle Door

Take your time with the thatched cottages
and ice-cream shops of Lulworth Cove before
continuing on to Durdle Door by boat or foot.
This natural limestone arch, formed more than
10,000 years ago, has become a symbol of the
Jurassic Coast and was England's very first
Natural World Heritage Site. The crystalline
water here (and at the neighbouring Man O'
War Beach) may be bracing, but it's worth
swimming beneath Durdle Door on a calm day.

Wareham BH20 5PU

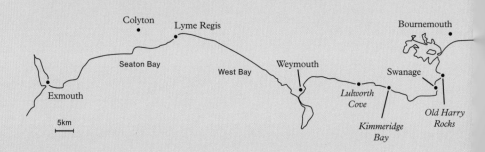

Glebe House

The Pig on the Beach

The Catch at the Old Fish Market

Lilac Restaurant & Wine Bar

Dorset House

NORFOLK

Go with the flow among marshes and dunes

Photographs by Tom Bunning

Whenever I need to unwind – let my shoulders drop and feel worries drift away – I head to the water. There's something about the rhythms and tides, the cyclical nature of it all, that comforts me. Sailing at sunset into Norfolk's Wells-next-the-Sea was no different. With the harbour millpond still, it was impossible to tell where the water ended and the pink, cloud-speckled August sky began. Our boat seemed to glide silently through a dreamscape.

With a 90-mile Coast Path, expansive beaches aplenty and around 23,000 ponds (more than any other English county), Norfolk is synonymous

with water – and those who call it home have a knack for building their lives and businesses around it. So naturally this is where I go when I need to switch off entirely and spend a weekend in muddy boots on, or beside, the water.

While the 125 miles of wildlife-rich waterways that make up the Norfolk Broads National Park are fascinating (home to windmills, abbey ruins and the walker-friendly towns of Woodbastwick and Ranworth), I based myself on Norfolk's dramatic north coast. My escape began in Wells-next-the-Sea, a port town known for its Victorian and Georgian architecture and hut-lined beach, which

Norfolk is synonymous with water – and those who call it home have a knack for building their lives and businesses around it

was where I set sail with The Coastal Exploration Company – our evening adventure culminating in that ethereal sunset.

The Coastal Exploration Company was founded in 2016 by ex-Royal Marine and humanitarian Henry Chamberlain, who takes immense delight in celebrating and preserving Norfolk's maritime past. The county's traditional fishing boats began to disappear rapidly in the 1960s and Henry's aim is to salvage and renovate as many of these old wooden vessels as he can, giving them a new life and promoting social and environmental change in the process. His fleet includes a mussel flat once used for gathering mussels from lays in the creeks, a larger crab boat that's able to venture further into the North Sea and a whelk boat, one of England's last, that was donated to him by a Brancaster fisherman. Sleek and silent with their tannin-hued sails unfurled, all these pre-loved craft are designed to immerse you fully in the seascape.

As we glided along the creeks aboard a mussel flat, the dark water a stark contrast to the pastel glow of the sea lavender, I spied the sculptural wooden stumps of long-lost bridges – remains from a time when these marshes were a series of interconnected islands used for grazing sheep. The major creeks don't shift much throughout the year, but the smaller run-offs and rivulets are prone to change so the Coastal Exploration team walk the banks and salterns once a year to recheck their routes. Stepping off to experience the spongy ground myself, watched by a curious

juvenile seal, I turned to see a second boat rounding a corner. From where I stood, it looked like little more than a single sail drifting across the flat, sage-and-olive-coloured terrain.

My skipper David sees expeditions like this as a way of championing a slower mode of travel – one that encourages a growing awareness of where you are in the world. But he's equally proud of their strong sustainability focus and the team's role as Norfolk custodians. The food they serve onboard is sourced from within 28 miles, they monitor and support wildlife and research and have even experimented with sailing cargo, moving Barsham Brewery's beer between Kings Lynn and Wells.

The following day, I travelled via Cley next the Sea (known for its windmill, pebble beach and pottery studio) to Holkham Hall, a lofty rural estate that's been home to the Coke family since the 17th century and is now dedicated to sustainable farming and land management. The Estate is also responsible for the Holkham National Nature Reserve, their 25,000 acres of grounds encompassing everything from salt marsh and dune-lined beaches to a walled garden that's being restored to its former 18th-century glory. Even here, the water takes centre-stage. There is a mile-long lake to cycle around as well as the beloved Holkham Beach, set in woodland and made famous by a fleeting yet memorable appearance in *Shakespeare in Love*. When the tide

(right) One of Settle's revamped vintage railway carriages

It's becoming clear that slow travel frequently shifts our outlook, and has a way of leaving us feeling stronger and more grounded than when we set off

is out, you can walk for miles across the sandy flats (or ride a horse); when it's in, the urge to swim is irresistible.

This sense of custodianship is something I also encountered further south, when I stayed in one of Settle's revamped vintage railway carriages, all of which are perched beside three lily-pad-strewn lakes. Settle is run by former floral-designer Jo Morfoot and her husband John, who re-dug the site's centuries-old, overgrown waterways with his father back in the 1970s. The couple rehabilitated the land, planted a forest (pairing exotic trees like sequoias and a Wollemi pine with native hornbeams, black poplars and elders) and built everything using salvaged materials. Their rustic, artful design sits in harmony with the wooded lakeside setting, and being here with the fires burning and the birds chattering feels like a reset – a reminder of how important it is for all of us, no matter where we live, to seek out time in nature.

Everyone I met in Norfolk takes something different from the water. For some, it's simply a calming backdrop, the water working its subtle magic without them being entirely aware. For others, it's a temporary reprieve: something to sail across or submerge in, a means of moving slower and with purpose, of noticing the tiny changes when travelling with the tides. And I'm starting to think that perhaps I take more from it than comfort, because after a weekend with these waterways I was left feeling unruffled and revived, ready to embrace whatever life threw at me, bolstered by memories of that late summer sunset.

It's becoming clear that slow travel (and being aboard a vintage fishing boat is nothing if not slow) frequently shifts our outlook, and has a way of leaving us feeling stronger and more grounded than when we set off. It's funny that we know travel can do this yet still need these reminders – these wild and unconventional experiences in nature reveal, again and again, how vital escape can be. If that's not a reason to set sail in Norfolk, then I don't know what is.

(overleaf) Sea lavender, an iconic feature of Norfolk salt marshes; Skipper David, from the Coastal Exploration Company, navigating the creeks near Wells-next-the-Sea

DIRECTORY

I spent most of my time exploring North Norfolk and its 45-mile-long coastline. But further south you'll also find the Broads National Park and Norwich, famous for its cathedral, independent galleries and canals.

STAY

The Gunton Arms

Owner and art dealer Ivor Braka has generously adorned The Gunton with millions of pounds worth of art from his private collection. You'll spy William Morris curtains, a Damian Hirst in the women's loo, the skull of a prehistoric elk dug up from a peat bog and a dining room bedecked in Tracy Emin's neon signs. As Ivor has famously explained, it costs a lot of money to look this cheap. Meals are as fabulous as the art and feature seasonal offerings like asparagus and wild garlic soup alongside staples such as Ivor's crab pasta, made using crustaceans caught off the neighbouring Cromer Beach. Much of the menu's brilliance comes down to its freshness, with venison sourced from the surrounding 1,000-acre deer park, and fruit and vegetables grown in their kitchen garden.

theguntonarms.co.uk
Norwich NR11 8TZ

Settle Norfolk

Enveloped by 30 acres of parkland, Settle is made up of a collection of converted railway carriages, cabins and safari tents that pop up in summer. Building materials hail from the owner's nearby Morways Reclamation, and the spaces are filled with handmade furnishings, vintage embellishments and custom pieces from English artisans. Round off your stay with a visit to the on-site shop, which brims with everything from Norfolk pottery to carved wooden platters.

settlenorfolk.co.uk
Larling Rd, Shropham, Attleborough NR17 1EA

The Brisley Bell

This is a proper country pub if ever there was one, complete with cosy nooks, Chesterfields and ancient fireplaces. But retreat to one of the bedrooms in the converted flint barn, and you'll find every contemporary comfort, including a freestanding bath ideal for post-sail soaks. Unwind in the snug bar and book-lined Garden Room restaurant, where the modern British menu changes daily.

thebrisleybell.co.uk
The Grn, Brisley, Dereham NR20 5DW

EAT

The Victoria Hotel and Restaurant

Part of the Holkham Estate, The Vic (as it's lovingly referred to by locals) is a hotel and restaurant with some serious foodie credentials. The decor is classic – antlers and rich wood, paired with a light-filled conservatory – and produce is grown in the Estate's expansive Georgian walled garden, keeping things both sustainable and scrumptious.

holkham.co.uk/welcome-to-the-victoria
Park Rd, Holkham, Wells-next-the-Sea NR23 1RG

The White Horse

Overlooking the marshland of Brancaster Staithe, this buzzing pub-meets-restaurant is devoted to hyper-local seafood. Oysters come from 700 yards away, fish are smoked on-site, marsh herbs are common accompaniments and mussels are gathered three bays over by fishermen who live a few doors down. The convivial atmosphere is bolstered by a programme of festivals, including ones dedicated to oysters, lobsters and sea shanties.

whitehorsebrancaster.co.uk
Main Rd, Brancaster Staithe, King's Lynn PE31 8BY

The Suffield Arms

The once-derelict Suffield Arms combines an old-world pub (built back in 1886 for those working on the Gunton Estate) with an art-adorned tapas restaurant. There's also an upstairs Saloon Bar, which is part boudoir, part drinking den, and looks like something from another era. Combining splashes of gold and velvet with carved wooden columns, this dashing space is made for romantic (and dare I say, debauched) nights.

suffieldarms.com
393 Station Rd, Lower Street, Norwich NR11 8UE

DO

Hindringham Hall

Built during the reigns of Henry VII and Henry VIII and surrounded by a 12th-century moat, the wisteria-covered Hindringham Hall is worth a gander for the architecture, but it's the gardens you should linger in. There's an ancient fishpond, a woodland walkway where Victorian ladies could saunter while avoiding the sun and an abundance of seasonal bulbs (bluebells and daffodils put on a show in late-April).

hindringhamhall.org
Blacksmiths Ln, Hindringham, Wells NR21 0QA

Blickling Hall

This castle-like Jacobite hall, cocooned within 5,000 acres of parkland, is a National Trust gem that stands beside The Bucks Arms, a petite 17th-century pub. Although there's no official documentation, many believe that The Hall is the birthplace of Anne Boleyn.

Blickling, Norwich NR11 6NF

Holkham Hall

Holkham Hall is the grande dame of Norfolk's stately homes, and was built by Thomas Coke, the first Earl of Leicester. Having inherited great wealth at just ten years of age, Thomas's ensuing rebellious teenage years were calmed by a six-year-long Grand Tour where he fell madly in love with Italy and its architecture. Visiting the Estate today, the Italian Palladian influence is immediately obvious in the Marble Hall: an imposing, column-and-statue-bedecked wedding cake of an entrance.

holkham.co.uk
Holkham Rd, Wells-next-the-Sea NR23 1AB

Settle Norfolk

Holkham Hall

The Gunton Arms

The Suffield Arms

The Brisley Bell

YORKSHIRE DALES

A road trip through grand ruins and green uplands

Photographs by Orlando Gili

We'd come to the Devil's Bridge in Kirkby Lonsdale, an arched stone behemoth dating from the 13th century, hoping to join the swimmers in the River Lune. But as my friend and I edged over the silvery rocks, summoning the courage to submerge, an approaching rain cloud stole my attention. The sky, which was a bright, unbroken blue just moments ago, was suddenly cast into shadow. Abandoning our adventure (I'll only swim if there's a possibility of sunning afterwards), we layered up and trudged back to the car. Our next destination, the highest pub in Britain, was a more appealing wet weather haunt.

Yet by the time we were back on the road, travelling along cliffside Buttertubs Pass (one of the country's best driving routes), the threat of rain had dissipated, and the bleakness was replaced by a dazzling pastel sunset. This was becoming a pattern on our journey through the Yorkshire Dales, and I still wasn't used to the speed at which the landscape changed, transitioning through every imaginable shade of green as clouds and the weather shifted with reckless abandon.

Our Yorkshire Dales odyssey began days earlier with an icon. Malham Cove may be well-known, but some sites (and the walking paths that lead

Floating on my back in the dappled pool at the fall's base,
my road-weary body was eased by the gasp-inducing cold

to them) are famous for a reason. One of the most photographed places in the National Park, this immense limestone amphitheatre is all that remains of a long-dried-up waterfall, with the grassy gorge over which it looms shaped by the river it once fed. From here, a circular trail (or ten-minute drive) delivers you to Gordale Scar, another narrow gorge that took shape over multiple Ice Ages. However you arrive, take the time to detour through the woods to Janet's Foss, a petite waterfall named for the queen of the fairies who, according to local lore, has made this glen her home. Floating on my back in the dappled pool at the fall's base, my road-weary body eased by the gasp-inducing cold, I could see why this quiet spot, near-hidden by rock and foliage, is entwined with the fantastic.

Further on, after leaving the car beside a road best suited to tractors, we tramped across fields under a peach-hued sky to Mastiles Lane, an ancient green road that drapes itself, almost ribbon-like, over the billowing, weather-worn terrain. Guarded by drystone walls, it looked entirely natural, as if it had been part of this landscape for aeons. In reality, it was once a Roman marching road, then repurposed as a drovers' route favoured by the monks of Fountains Abbey. These days it is a fell walker's dream.

Take a road trip through the Dales and you'll be travelling with history. The terrain itself is made up of limestone (formed from ancient sea

creatures, the fossils of shells and coral still visible in the rock), and the route is peppered with ruined abbeys, hallowed drinking dens and the scars and marks of settlers past. This rang true the following day when the drive to Grassington (a picturesque village that doubled as the fictional market town of Doarrowby in the TV series *All Creatures Great and Small*) took us past Bolton Abbey, a ruined Augustinian priory by the wild-swimming-friendly River Wharfe. Surrounded by 80 miles of footpaths, Bolton set the day's mood perfectly – how better to prepare yourself for antiques and heirlooms than by spending a morning appreciating an abbey's skeletal stone remains?

We were in Grassington to meet Rob Cain, who is better known as The English Polisher. Rob is a second-generation French polisher, which is the traditional art of applying shellac to furniture to preserve and restore it. Rob learnt the skill from his father, working alongside him in old houses and churches in exchange for pocket money – and you'll likely pass his work as you travel across the Dales, although he happily goes uncredited for most of it. As a guerrilla polisher, he'll pull up at a church, notice that a door or bench needs some love and set about polishing it – all at his own expense and usually under the cover of darkness. During the day, he runs classes from his high street workshop, ideal for those who long to be artists but struggle when it comes to the detail; as Rob points out, even if you aren't amazing at drawing, you can always do something with a bit of furniture. The space is filled with a melange of antique curiosities, from signs and letterpress

(left) Janet's Foss waterfall
(overleaf) Malham Cove; Rob Cain, the English Polisher

Take a road trip through the Dales and you'll be travelling with history

stamps to a barn owl sculpted from wire. This assortment is a testament to the fact that heirlooms don't need to be expensive; they just need to come with meaning and memories, which the restoration process can help revive.

Enlivened by abbeys and antiques (and with our hopes of that Devil's Bridge swim dashed), we continued driving north to Tan Hill Inn, the aforementioned tavern with the grand title of 'highest pub in Britain'. Here, the landscape opens up. Ancient stone walls snake their way over fells, catching the honey-hued light of golden hour, which illuminates the scenic scattering of abandoned stone houses. Down south, the landscape hugs you once again. Hills feel close, valleys appear steeper and forests thrive, protected from the winter winds that blast the northern moorland.

But no matter where you are in the Dales, you're constantly taken by surprise. Set out for an icon like Malham Cove, and you'll likely lose an entire afternoon wandering through woodland so lush it could be mistaken for rainforest. Prepare for a swim and instead spend the evening watching the most dazzling sunset imaginable.

The closer we came to Tan Hill Inn, following a single-lane road cloaked in fern and scattered with sheep, the quieter we became. We needed the silence to take the landscape in and make sure we held on to this feeling of awe. With crumbling abbeys and historic train journeys ahead of us, we knew more beauty awaited – but that made it all the more important to appreciate the world before us, until the scene changed again.

(right) The Devil's Bridge in Kirkby Lonsdale, a 13th-century structure over the River Lune

DIRECTORY

To follow our route, spend your first night feasting at The Angel at Hetton, then journey on to Malham Cove, Bolton Abbey and Grassington. Spend your second night at Stow House, taking a circular route past the Devil's Bridge and Tan Hill Inn, before heading on to Middleton Lodge. As with any road trip, leave room for unexpected discoveries.

STAY

Stow House

It's all about the detail in this restored vicarage turned B&B, a short drive from Jervaulx Abbey. There are four-poster beds, immense sash windows with views out across the rolling Wensleydale hills, antique wardrobes, clawfooted tubs, velvet lounges and an arresting collection of artworks including a Victorian skylight reimagined as a feature wall. The design is clearly inspired by convivial owners Sarah and Phil Bucknall's time in the London advertising world and the couple also have a flair for throwing parties, in case you have a celebration on the horizon.

stowhouse.co.uk
Stow House, Leyburn DL8 3SR

Middleton Lodge

If you want to continue on to the North Yorkshire Moors (home to Robin Hood's Bay and Whitby Abbey, which inspired Bram Stoker's *Dracula*) spend a night relaxing between the two National Parks at Middleton Lodge, a 200-acre Georgian country estate found on the edge of the Yorkshire Dales. The Coach House – one of the hotel's two lauded restaurants – has built its low-food-mile menu around ingredients grown in the two-acre kitchen garden. Bedrooms are found in the original Coach House, Walled Garden, Orchard and Dairy, although you'll want to spend most of your time at the Forest Spa. This decadent space features a heated outdoor pool and woodland-scented thermal spa.

middletonlodge.co.uk
Kneeton Ln, Middleton Tyas, Richmond DL10 6NJ

EAT

The Craven Arms

Follow hungry hikers to this 16th-century pub famed for its ferret racing and annual conkers championship. Owner David Ainsworth is in his 80s but still pulls pints behind the bar (Appletreewick Cider is brewed 100 yards down the road), and The Cavern's stone walls and nooks are decorated with his collection of vintage treasures.

craven-cruckbarn.mobi
Appletreewick, Skipton BD23 6DA

Tan Hill Inn

Standing at 1,732 feet above sea level, the character-attracting, laid-back 17th-century Tan Hill Inn (replete with 360-degree views and an immense fire that you'd like to imagine is always burning) is found at the end of Buttertubs Pass. This scenic road is named for the limestone holes dotted along the route that were once used by farmers to keep their butter cool when heading down to the market town of Hawes.

tanhillinn.com
Long Causeway, Richmond DL11 6ED

The Angel at Hetton

A sleek and welcoming Michelin-starred restaurant with rooms five miles from Grassington, The Angel's design is elegantly refined: a creative mix of timber, stone and earthy hues, paired with a statement moss-covered wall that ensures the Dales are never far from your mind. Chef patron Michael Wignall's menu is influenced by flavours from across the globe, and while the dishes are brilliantly complex (they all arrived looking like sculptural works of art), this is balanced by the sheer freshness of every ingredient, flavours changing with each bite. Stay the night to experience the spacious Scandi-esque bedrooms and sensational, multi-course breakfast.

angelhetton.co.uk
Back Ln, Hetton, Skipton BD23 6LT

DO

Settle to Carlisle Railway

Crossing the Pennines, the 73-mile-long Settle to Carlisle line opened in 1876 and was built almost entirely by hand. Full of valleys and viaducts like oft-photographed Ribblehead with its 24 towering stone arches, this is one for train enthusiasts and scenery lovers alike.

settle-carlisle.co.uk

Abbey Ruins

Thanks to Henry VIII's Dissolution of the Monasteries in the 1530s, Yorkshire has a superb collection of religious ruins. Bolton Abbey is a Dales gem and North Yorkshire's Fountains Abbey is UNESCO-protected, yet the lesser explored Jervaulx has its own quiet power.

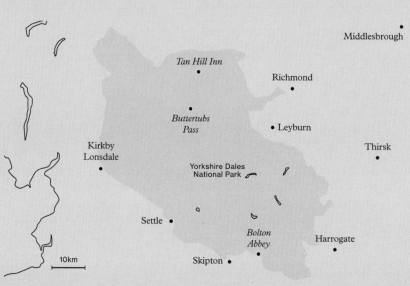

The Craven Arms

Stow House

Middleton Lodge

The Angel at Hetton

Settle to Carlisle Railway

Middleton Lodge

NEW FOREST

Find sanctuary in England's ancient woodland

Photographs by Daisy Wingate-Saul

Time in nature has always been one of the best ways to slow down. Walking through a forest, we're aware of our body's rhythms, the shifts in our breathing, the feel of sunlight on our skin, the sound of leaves crunching underfoot. Put us near the ebb and flow of water and things become truly meditative. But transitioning from an everyday, madcap being to a chilled-out, nature-embracing traveller can be a challenge – especially when the world around us feels particularly charged. To ease this change, it sometimes helps to seek out a little luxury. A massage, a long lunch, breakfast served among the treetops – all encourage you to

move at a far more leisurely pace. Adventure and beauty may be good for the soul, but so is treating yourself. And when it comes to doing the latter (while enveloped by woodland and water), few places are quite as inviting as the New Forest.

Created in 1079 as royal hunting grounds for William the Conqueror, the folklore-filled New Forest transports you to the England of old, a collage of heath, greenwood, heather, moorland and gorse. Head out from any of its stone villages, the ground below you softened by moss and decades of fallen leaves, and you'll walk beneath oaks, yews and elms bent every which way in their search for

I watched the hotel's beekeeper tend to the hives, methodically checking the honeycomb, every movement measured, masterful and assured

sunlight and space. What's staggering, though, is just how fast the landscape changes, shifting from forest to meadow, heath to quaint hamlets where ponies halt traffic and gardens are guarded by cattle grates – although the fight to protect foliage from peckish bovine neighbours appears futile. This is one of the last places in England where common grazing is still practiced, with a small group of people (many of whom come from families who have been 'commoning' for generations) able to access the land for grazing, an activity that has helped shape this terrain over the centuries and is now built into the National Park's management programme.

And throughout this ancient, semi-natural woodland (a once common habitat that now covers only two per cent of England) are lavish boltholes that beckon to gourmands and spa-devotees alike. Chewton Glen, Lime Wood and The Pig in particular prove that here, there is so much more than wilderness.

Chewton Glen is a New Forest grande dame, an old-world country hotel with heart. There's retro wallpaper and ornate plasterwork, light-filled treehouse rooms where you can forest bathe from an outdoor hot tub and 130 acres of grounds. Visit in summer and the walled garden is a melange of artichokes and sweet peas, while cocktails are served in the courtyard surrounded by an explosion of

(left) The beekeeper at The Pig. The hives are part of the hotel's Kitchen Garden, producing raw, unpasteurised and unprocessed honey

lavender. To really embrace the slower pace, head to the spa, where you can daydream in the sun-drenched pool, have worries massaged away or bob from jet to jet in the hydrotherapy pool, one of Europe's largest.

But even when enveloped in so much opulence, the forest remains ever-present and all-encompassing. At the end of a field of apple trees and beehives is a dense canopy twittering with birdsong, and from the terrace, overlooking a kaleidoscope of green, it feels as if the wilderness is calling you. To answer this siren's song, wander past the outdoor pool and croquet pitch, through a gate and on into the hazel and holly-filled Chewton Bunny – a wooded ravine (that's part of a wider nature reserve) once popular with New Forest smugglers. The path ends at Highcliffe Beach, and as you stand and gaze from the pebbled shore, you can see the Isle of Wight's glowing cliffs, the watery scene a world away from the woodland you've just left.

Part of the New Forest's old-world charm is its four-legged inhabitants, some of whom have called the area home for around 2,000 years. I saw my first New Forest pony just outside the quaint market town of Lyndhurst. I was walking through heather and gorse speckled moorland when it emerged, seemed to look me up and down, and then continued calmly on its way – clearly used to human admirers. You can see why these animals are often thought of as wild. But while they are free roaming and semi-feral (don't go in for a pat), the ponies – along with cattle and donkeys – are part of the commoning programme. Their grazing has allowed plants like chamomile and gladiolus to thrive, while keeping scrubland at bay.

I'd come to Lyndhurst to unwind at Lime Wood, a Georgian hunting lodge turned luxury, 33-room hotel bordered by undulating heath. While the art-filled space is heavenly, the Herb House Spa is the star, and features a hydrotherapy pool that looks out over a swathe of forest, reminiscent of Japanese *onsen* (hot spring). An assortment of hiking and biking trails begin at the hotel's door, and while an aimless meander through the heather may be enough to transport you, there are longer walks for the intrepid. The 8.5-mile Lyndhurst Parish Walk takes in ponies and sculptural yews at the view-boasting Bolton's Bench, and the relatively flat, tree-lined trail to Brockenhurst suits both cyclists and ramblers (travel quietly here as it will increase your chance of spotting foraging deer). Although it's a circular journey, you can also draw the walk to a close at The Pig – the ideal place to end a hedonistic New Forest odyssey.

Originally built as a Groom Keepers' Lodge to house the men hired to protect wood supplies and ward off poachers when the forest was used for timber production in the 17th and 18th centuries, The Pig is now the ultimate restaurant with rooms. History lingers in the uniquely shaped rooms, the vintage adornments and the cocktail lounge's salvaged altar-turned-bar. The latter's ornate woodwork is balanced by multi-coloured glassware, the ideal receptacles for experimental cocktails made with ingredients like pear-infused gin, lavender tinctures and vodka spiced with garden-grown chilli. In keeping with the hotel's sustainable ethos, every cocktail includes at least one element from The Pig's Kitchen Garden – which is also home to a Victorian greenhouse, quails, duck ponds and beehives. Walking here in the early evening, the clouds low and the light soft, I watched the hotel's beekeeper tend to the hives, methodically checking the honeycomb, every movement measured, masterful and assured. The grasses around us were high, and the fruit trees swayed gently in the breeze. I don't know it if was due to the setting, her confidence or the culmination of a lush weekend, but the buzz that at first seemed cacophonous soon struck me as a soothing, melodic hum.

While travelling, there's often a compulsion to tick things off a list: to climb, swim, ramble and experience something entirely new. Sometimes, though, the ultimate reset comes from simply indulging – in lounging by a pool, dressing up for dinner and taking the time to admire a sunset, with a woodland-inspired cocktail in hand. And it's the chance to savour such lavishness in a wild and wonderful natural backdrop that will keep me coming back to the New Forest.

(right) The Dining Room, Chewton Glen, famed for its classic, French-inspired menu

DIRECTORY

The New Forest is especially beautiful in spring when bluebells cover the forest floor. This is also the season for spotting foals – just remember to keep a safe distance from the ponies as they are protective of their young.

STAY & EAT

Chewton Glen Hotel & Spa

Found at the southern edge of the New Forest, this regal hotel (part of the Relais & Châteaux group and famed for its spa and family-friendly ethos) is also known for its exceptional food. The Dining Room offers a classic, French-inspired menu (they have served their cheese soufflé for more than 30 years), while the garden-adjacent restaurant, the Kitchen, has copper tables are designed to show the marks of every meal that has come before, the artful splatters hinting at past decadence.

For a memorable stay, book one of their self-contained, open-plan treehouses. Here, you can stargaze from an outdoor hot tub (or simply admire the scene from bed), and breakfast hampers arrive at your room via a secret hatch so you can feast on exceptional fare from your private balcony overlooking a sea of green.

chewtonglen.com
Christchurch Rd, New Milton BH25 6QS

Lime Wood

Lime Wood is a hotel that transports you. The skylight-illuminated bar, all marble and statement fabrics, feels very LA. The scullery, used each morning for breakfast, is decidedly Scottish (as is the on-site smokery), while the jasmine-draped walkways seem perfectly Italian. Add an eclectic array of contemporary art and the Herb House Spa, and you have a setting you can't really tear yourself away from – no matter how cute the neighbouring ponies might be.

Lime Wood's star is Hartnett Holder & Co, a dazzling showpiece restaurant from chefs Angela Hartnett and Luke Holder. With Hampshire's natural larder guiding the Tuscan-meets-New-Forest menu, it's unlikely two meals will ever be quite the same. My own dinner captured the flavours of summer – lobster linguine; pickled apricots and buratta with a lemon verbena zing; and heritage tomatoes balanced by mozzarella cream. Everything is pure, delicious alchemy.

limewoodhotel.co.uk
Beaulieu Rd, Lyndhurst SO43 7FZ

The Pig

In keeping with the New Forest tradition, food is at the heart of this charming Brockenhurst hotel dedicated to promoting local and home-grown produce. When gathering ingredients from beyond the garden (the domain of the eponymous pigs), the kitchen team aim to source everything from within a 25-mile radius and even employ a full-time forager. The scrumptious results are dished up in the conservatory restaurant, an artful collage of mismatched furniture and retro crockery. Seasonal menu highlights during my stay included a phenomenal gooseberry tart and a raspberry cheesecake whose consistency appeared to defy the laws of physics.

thepighotel.com
Beaulieu Rd, Brockenhurst, Hampshire, SO42 7QL

DO

Beaulieu

For chocolate box quaintness, visit Beaulieu, an enchanting town filled with donkeys and tea shops, and the site of Beaulieu Estate, where Sir Arthur Conan Doyle once tried to banish a disgruntled spirit. The Estate now houses the National Motor Museum and marks the start of the walk to Buckler's Hard, an 18th-century shipyard village where the ships used by Nelson at the Battle of Trafalgar were built.

Lymington

A Georgian seaside town known for its cobbled streets, Saturday market and Sea Water Baths, historic Lymington sits on the Solent Straight and is a great place to set sail for the Isle of Wight. Once on the island, you can search for dinosaur fossils, follow the Monk Walk or admire The Needles, chalk sea stacks that look like a submerged dragon's back.

Into the woods

With more than 140 miles of deer-dotted walking and cycling trails, it's easy to get adventurous in the New Forest. Hire a bike from the family-run Cyclexperience in Brockenhurst (the team also supply local maps with fab pubs and views marked) or take part in a guided adventure with New Forest Cycling Tours.

Alternatively, you could enjoy a meditative spell of forest bathing. The idea is to focus on the details around you – the scent, the feel of the earth beneath your feet, the way the sunlight filters through foliage – and allow your mind to still. The simple act of walking among trees has been proven to lower stress, anxiety and blood pressure, boost moods and do wonders for our immune systems.

Beaulieu Estate

The Pig

ime Wood

Lime Wood

The Kitchen, Chewton Glen

me Wood

Lymington

CORNWALL

Discover a land through its art

Photographs by Daisy Wingate-Saul

Cornwall's artistic heritage is the stuff of legend. The county has been a haven for artists for centuries – the Impressionist-inspired Newlyn School emerged in the 1880s and the Falmouth School of Art opened in 1902 – but things really kicked off when a pioneering group of practitioners arrived in St Ives after the First World War craving space, sea and light. United by a fascination with abstraction and a desire to capture the region's allure, they established the St Ives School, an art colony that was at its height in the 1950s and '60s. It became a hub of British modernism, attracting the likes of all-round

artistic icon Barbara Hepworth and ceramicist Bernard Leach, who has been praised for elevating pottery to an art form. Today, their output is celebrated in Tate St Ives, perched above Porthmeor Beach, and a collection of beautifully preserved studios.

Entering Leach's studio-turned-museum, you'd be forgiven for thinking you'd stumbled back in time. Clay-speckled and serene, the space is left as he would have had it, although kilns now brim with tableware from the Leach Standard Ware Range which is inspired by his organic, earthy originals. Leach moved to St Ives in 1920 and

founded Leach Pottery with Shōji Hamada, who was designated a Living National Treasure for his contribution to studio pottery in Japan, where the two artists met. Leach's pieces – many of which were inspired by Cornish mythology and *chanoyu*, the traditional tea ceremony – were created using a Japanese-style climbing kiln, the first of its kind in England.

A journey through St Ives' artistic history would be incomplete without a visit to the Barbara Hepworth Museum and Sculpture Garden, an open-air oasis built around Hepworth's Trewyn Studio. St Ives is a knot of steep, busy lanes and whitewashed cottages, but this sculpture garden feels like a haven and offers a glimpse into how Hepworth lived and worked. Her sculptures, made from wood, bronze and stone, are both abstract responses to the landscape and musings on the universal human experience – attempts to capture feelings rather than reality. Seeing them dotted among tropical flowers, with neighbouring church bells tolling the hour, the thrum of seaside St Ives in high summer falls away. All these years later, the peace and splendour that called those early practitioners to Cornwall remains.

I met ceramicist Sam Marks, who is acutely aware of the region's artistic heritage, in Falmouth – a university town about an hour's drive from St Ives. 'Historically, Cornwall had a very embedded, rich art history, and a lot of the artists who moved here are still very revered,' he explains. 'On the back of that, you'll get generations of people being inspired by their work. Clearly the coast resonates with artists as well. It's a beautiful landscape to paint and draw experience from. It's also very mineral-rich, which is great for potters and those working with natural pigments. And there's an energy, especially when it comes to the water. The tide retreating and coming back every day, that changes the atmosphere in the towns. It's something you can't quantify; you can't really label – it's just a feeling.'

(left) Ceramicist Sam Marks in his Falmouth studio
(overleaf) Work by Olivia Lucy Bush, a printmaker inspired by the Cornish seascape; Bedruthan Steps, found along the South West Coast Path

Sam works from a studio above Morgan's Gallery, just one of the spaces – alongside Falmouth Art Gallery and the North Coast Asylum in Newquay – dedicated to exhibiting Cornish artists. Looking at his coast-inspired sculptures, I saw a connection to Hepworth's natural, free-flowing forms. 'Sometimes I call them negative space forms, sometimes I call them erosion pieces,' Sam says of his creations. 'They're intended to represent the sensation of holding a polished pebble on the beach.' Eyeing one of his pieces, made using harvested clay, I was struck by how lovely it is that such nuanced, skilled work can represent something so simple.

People have long praised Cornwall's light, and I suspect the salt-diffused softness has a part to play in the tranquillity that permeates a lot of local artworks. This is true of self-taught printmaker Olivia Lucy Bush's work, which I first spied in Beside The Wave, a gallery in Falmouth. With a penchant for 'capturing quiet things', her style is rooted in the natural world, which is fitting given that the landscape – and the sea in particular – drew Olivia to Cornwall. 'Living here is so special,' she says of her home just outside Truro. 'You're ten minutes from the beach. And as my studio is part of a working farm, you're in the seasons, in the weather. You can't escape it. Nature leads your day.'

Being outdoors is part of Olivia's practice. She'll head to the cliffs, sketch in the wild, then return to the studio to create her prints, treating the entire process like a private residency. 'Walking along the Coast Path near St Agnes, the landscape looks like it did hundreds of years ago. It's pretty special because the world is so complex, but when you're on the Path or in the water, time becomes irrelevant. We can get so bogged down with life in a busy world that it's nice to walk somewhere that hasn't changed.'

Printmaker Mimi Robson is equally besotted with the waves and is fascinated by how the environment can reflect our own sense of self – and the way our moods and energies may change as much as the weather. Like our complex inner worlds, she wants her dreamy, layered etchings

Perhaps that's ultimately what Cornwall offers –
scenery that jolts you out of the everyday, an irresistible
combination of waves, light, cliffs and space

to appear simple at first glance, revealing more of themselves the longer you look.

Chatting to Mimi in her Newquay studio, I realised that one of the most striking things about Cornwall's art scene is just how tight-knit the community is. Everyone seems keen to praise each other's work and talk honestly about the realities of leading a creative life – and the joy of sharing a common muse. Regardless of the medium they use, every artist I spoke to was in awe of this environment. 'Cornwall's artistic history is tied to the rawness of the coastline – and the light is magic, you can see it in the landscape works,' Mimi says. 'It's such a narrow piece of land and you feel close to water wherever you are. There's a saltiness in the air, it's all very raw. That's what I'm drawn to.'

For most of my trip, I stayed at Kudhva, a glamping-site-meets-landscape-hotel run by Louise Middleton. Waking up immersed in woodland, with the sea visible on the horizon, helped me understand Cornwall's artistic allure. When getting creative, our minds need room to roam, to feel removed from the safe and familiar,

and the self-imposed limitations that brings. Walking from my cabin each morning through a maze of twisted willow, past carpets of dog violets and wild strawberries, and looking out across heathland to the coast, I could feel ideas start to bloom. 'I'm interested in people doing their best work,' says Louise, when explaining what she hoped to create at Kudhva. 'They can either bring work with them or they can totally relax, feel inspired, and then go away having had a shift of consciousness. We all need perspective, and you need quite big incremental shifts to let that happen. It makes you feel inspired and alive. Nature will do that immediately because the veil between indoors and outdoors is so fine.'

Perhaps that's ultimately what Cornwall offers – scenery that jolts you out of the everyday, an irresistible combination of waves, light, cliffs and space. And being in the presence of a sublime, changeable landscape is clearly doing wonders for the next generation of makers, who were drawn to the artistic pedigree and stayed for something wilder.

(previous) The Leach Pottery, founded by Bernard Leach and Shōji Hamada in 1920; Newquay-based printmaker Mimi Robson

DIRECTORY

*Come to Cornwall for the art, but stay for the food, boltholes and seascapes. With
a lot of ground to cover, hiring a car is a great option, and if you're travelling from
London you can arrive in Penzance aboard the Night Riviera Sleeper train service.*

STAY

Watergate Bay Hotel
Nestled beneath a headland with uninterrupted views of the Atlantic's waves, this family-friendly hotel is made for beach-lovers. Inside, a classic English seaside hotel has been elevated by modern, airy extensions. There is an artful abundance of beach paraphernalia, an on-site surf school, soothing spa, a pool that hovers above the sand and a collection of excellent bars and restaurants – the après-surf culture here is strong. For a room with a jaw-dropping view, book a Beach Loft: a spacious, impeccably designed abode with floor-to-ceiling windows and a perfectly positioned roll-top bath that allows you to watch the retreating tide change the scene entirely. And while it may be tempting to spend your entire getaway at Watergate Bay, make sure you visit Bedruthan Steps, a gorgeous cove along the South West Coast Path.

watergatebay.co.uk
On the beach, Watergate Bay TR8 4AA

Botelet
This historic farmhouse (in the Tamblyn family for more than 150 years) has been renovated into a collection of charming holiday cottages, from the Grade II-listed Manor Cottage to a cosy yurt perfect for summer nights. Co-owner Tia Tamblyn – who hosts a podcast series shining a light on local producers – has far-flung Cornish recommendations aplenty, but also understands the appeal of staying near Botelet: 'With the beaches and moors so close, there's a slowness that envelopes you. There's a culture of taking the time to go for a sea swim, to embrace the elements in so many different ways. It's all about having the room to breathe.'

botelet.com
Herodsfoot, Liskeard PL14 4RD

Kudhva
Made up of site-specific architectural hideouts nested in deciduous woodland, Kudhva (which is Cornish for hideout) also includes a wood-burning hot tub, waterfall, restored engine house and abandoned slate quarry. Design enthusiasts will be charmed by the Kudhva cabins themselves – contemporary, treehouse-like structures with a mezzanine sleeping area made for stargazing. This is raw-luxe at its finest and exists because of owner Louise's desire to 'make friends with the land', which she transformed from a wild and forgotten space into this off-grid event- and festival-hosting bolthole.

kudhva.com
Sanding Rd, Trebarwith Strand, Tintagel,
*   Cornwall PL34 0HH*

EAT

Temple
Bude is known for its sea pool, brilliant beaches and Temple, a family-run restaurant and wine bar where an innovative, seasonal focus and a passion for phenomenal Cornish ingredients means that you'll remember these dishes (which are constantly changing and designed to be shared) long after the meal has ended.

templecornwall.com
10 Granville Ter, Bude EX23 8JZ

The Rocket Store
In Boscastle, found along a stretch of the Coast Path steeped in Arthurian legend, this petite restaurant is rightly hailed as a local gem serving some of the freshest seafood around. The menu evolves depending on what the owner catches that day, and the vibe is electric.

therocketstore.co.uk
The Harbour, Boscastle PL35 0HD

Potager Garden
Once an abandoned plant nursery, Potager Garden is now a vegetarian cafe set within a thriving greenhouse. With attached artist studios and a range of workshops and events, it's a space where creativity has free rein.

potagergarden.org
High Cross, Constantine, Falmouth TR11 5RF

The Beach Hut, Watergate Bay Hotel
Suspended above Watergate Bay and open from morning to night, the laid-back Beach Hut is a hallowed post-surf haunt. Breakfasts are long and half the menu is plant-based. Cocktails capture the flavours of summer, and the restaurant proves that fish and chips (and moules marinière) taste better when you can see the sea.

watergatebay.co.uk/food-drink/the-beach-hut
On the beach, Watergate Bay, TR8 4AA

DO

Lost Gardens of Heligan
Comprising 200 undulating acres of cultivated gardens and woodland, Heligan lay forgotten after the First World War (which claimed the lives of 16 of its 22 gardeners) until Tim Smith (the man behind the Eden Project) rediscovered it by accident in the '90s. Already divine, the space is being lovingly restored to its former blooming glory.

heligan.com
Pentewan, Saint Austell PL26 6EN

Minack Theatre
While artistic respects should be paid to the Art Deco Jubilee Pool and Tremenheere Sculpture Gardens in Penzance, be sure to linger at the open air Minack Theatre, which is built into the cliff above Porthcurno Bay. Created in 1932 by thespian Rowena Cade, seats in this Greek-style theatre are adorned with carvings of the names of past productions. Performances still run from Easter to October, the ocean a suitably dramatic backdrop.

minack.com
Porthcurno, Penzance TR19 6JU

The Leach Pottery Museum
The original home and workplace of Bernard Leach, this museum charts the (still working) studio's 100-year history and hosts a range of exhibitions.

leachpottery.com
Higher Stennack, Saint Ives TR26 2HE

Barbara Hepworth Museum and Sculpture Garden
Hepworth lived and worked in Trewyn Studio until her death in 1975, and the site's sculpture garden remains a Cornish icon.

tate.org.uk/visit/tate-st-ives/barbara-hepworth-
*   museum-and-sculpture-garden*
Barnoon Hill, Saint Ives TR26 1AD

Barbara Hepworth Museum and Sculpture Garden

Kudhva

Botelet's Manor Cottage

The Beach Hut at Watergate Bay Hotel

Rocket Store

Temple

BATH

Relax in an ancient spa town

Photographs by Leon Foggitt

Never underestimate the bliss of a bath – although be aware that not all soaks are created equal. For thousands of years, people have been drawn to thermal waters, enamoured not only with their healing powers but by how soothed they feel after a dip. Geothermal springs have been embraced across the globe, with the ancient Greeks and Romans 'taking the waters' to treat everything from arthritis to skin conditions, viewing these natural baths as sacred places thanks to the apparent miracles the water performed. There is a rich bathing heritage in England too, shaped by both Celtic and Roman traditions. To experience this, it's best to board a train to Bath.

Today, Bath is a UNESCO-protected city celebrated for a multitude of riches, most notably its Georgian architecture (highlights include The Circus, Royal Crescent and Pump Room) and Roman remains (the most striking of which is the centrally located bath complex itself). It was the Romans who first put Bath (then Aquae Sulis) on the ancient spa town map, although early Britons had been embracing Bath's hot springs long before that. Geoffrey of Monmouth (the 12th-century monk and somewhat inaccurate historian who

made King Arthur famous) even wrote that Bladud, the King of the Britons, was cured of leprosy after bathing (and falling asleep) in the warm mud around the spring – something he decided to try after noticing that it had healed his pigs the previous day. The account is unreliable, but a statue of Bladud (who, once recovered, went on to assume the Crown) overlooks the Cross Bath, an open-air thermal pool built from honeyed stone that can be hired for group or solo experiences.

Every day, Bath's springs (now named King's Bath, Hetling and Cross Baths) pump more than one million litres of hot water (temperatures can reach 46°C), which is packed with minerals and elements including magnesium, sulphate, silica, calcium, sodium and iron. It takes the water around 12,000 years to travel from its source, somewhere in the surrounding limestone hills – this journey is long and arduous as rainwater needs to seep through the earth's surface and travel to a depth of roughly 1.25 miles before the natural heating process even begins.

One of the best ways to bathe in Bath today is to swan around Thermae Bath Spa in the city's historic centre. The two pools of this complex are fed by all three springs and, when bobbing here, you catch yourself wondering over the mysterious subterranean workings that have unfolded to make a morning of soporific floating such a pleasure. Isn't that the old adage, that good things come to those who wait? Thermae's Wellness Suite, with its mix of saunas and relaxation spaces, reflects Bath's past, with a Roman-inspired steam room that features a mosaic of Sulis Minerva – a union of the Celtic Sulis and Minerva, the Roman goddess of commerce, poetry and the arts (the empire had a knack for adopting and appropriating endemic beliefs). The Georgian steam room has sculptured windows framing frescoes of garden

scenes and the Relaxation Room, with its celestial ceiling, honours Caroline and William Herschel, who were in Bath when they accidentally discovered the planet Uranus in 1781. Thermae's rooftop pool overlooks the Grade I-listed Bath Abbey, a sacred site for more than a millennia. Stained glass and fan vaulting aside, I've always adored the Green Man figure carved into one of the pews (a Pagan symbol thought to herald the arrival of spring) and the stone angels climbing up and down a ladder by the Abbey's entrance.

Contemporary Bath is compact, the Abbey standing right beside the original Roman Baths and Georgian Pump Room (now a restaurant famed for its afternoon tea). From here, amble (via a network of shop-lined alleys) to The Circus and Royal Crescent, some of the country's most recognisable architectural gems. Alternatively, cross over the Palladian-style Pulteney Bridge, pop into The Holburne Museum, stroll through Sydney Gardens (England's last remaining 18th-century pleasure garden) and reach the canal, another watery delight.

Given that Bath is one of UNESCO's 11 Great Spa Towns of Europe, you should treat it with the respect it deserves and arrive in style – it's what those Regency-era writers, royals and artists would have done. The British Pullman, A Belmond Train, rolls along various routes across England, giving passengers a taste of travel as it once was – a window into a time when you dressed up and found pleasure in taking the slow route. On board, marquetry woodwork is de rigueur, and it's remarkably easy to embrace the unhurried pace while imbibing English sparkling wine and watching the countryside roll by. This vintage extravaganza perfectly prepares you for taking Bath's mineral-rich waters, which still feels like a decadent, spiritual experience.

(left) Pulteney Weir
(overleaf) The Cross Bath, an open-air thermal bath at Thermae Bath Spa; The Gainsborough Bath Spa

DIRECTORY

Once you've taken the waters and admired the brilliant architecture, draw out your Bath experience by escaping into nature – the striking Cheddar Gorge (and its caves) is less than an hour's drive away.

STAY

The Gainsborough Bath Spa

Named in honour of the artist who called Bath home for a time, this hotel sits within a restored 18th-century building in the city's heart. During construction, 17,500 Roman silver coins were unearthed, some of which are on display in the lobby. The design is dapper, the interiors filled with marble, plush beds and period-inspired furnishings. The cocktail bar is a delight and afternoon tea is a refined affair, but the standout is their Spa Village, which is fed by Bath's ancient mineral springs, the natural healing properties of the water boosted by a range of lush treatments.

thegainsboroughbathspa.co.uk
Beau St, Bath BA1 1QY

Lucknam Park Hotel & Spa

Look to this stately country hotel for a secluded escape, just six miles from Bath surrounded by woodland and fields. There are many reasons to book a stay – the lavish rooms, the 500 acres of listed parkland (home to deer, horses, sculptures and numerous walking paths), the Michelin-starred Restaurant Hywel Jones (that has held its star since 2006) and the spa, which features one of the most picturesque pools in the country. This is old-world England: a hotel elevated by Georgian architecture, an antiques-filled library made for cocktail-sipping, a blooming walled garden and a mile-long entrance lined with 200-year-old lime and beech trees.

lucknampark.co.uk
Lucknam Park, Chippenham SN14 8AZ

EAT

Corkage

Specialising in small plates and international wines (there are more than 120 bottles on the menu), Corkage takes tipples very seriously. Feasting unfolds in the wood-and-leather-filled restaurant, beneath the covered terrace or in their courtyard garden, and a team of wine aficionados are on hand if you want to shop.

corkagebath.com
5 Chapel Row, Bath BA1 1HN

Beckford Bottle Shop

Take your time at this Chesterfield-filled Saville Row wine bar, found near the Bath Assembly Rooms. There are regular wine tastings and events, and while the small plates are delicious, you can walk downhill for a feast at Beckford Canteen if you're after something more substantial.

beckfordbottleshop.com
5-8 Saville Row, Bath BA1 2QP

The Scallop Shell

Things feel perfectly relaxed at the family-run Scallop Shell, a convivial restaurant with a flair for fruits de mer – much of which is on display in an ice-filled bathtub by the entrance. This is where you come for some of the country's best sustainably caught fish and chips.

thescallopshell.co.uk
22 Monmouth Pl, Bath BA1 2AY

DO

Take the Waters

A wonderful way to bathe is to book a stay at The Gainsborough or unwind at Thermae Bath Spa. Alternatively, embrace history at the astoundingly well-preserved Roman Baths (join a Bath Abbey Tower Tour for an aerial view). If you're feeling active, head to the Bath Boating Station and punt down the River Avon or stroll along the canal all the way to the lofty Dundas Aqueduct.

Bookshops

As befits its long literary history, Bath is a city filled with bookshops. George Bayntun specialises in bookbinding and antique tomes, Magalleria stocks almost every indie magazine ever made and Topping & Company Booksellers of Bath is a bookworms' oasis, dotted with snug reading nooks. Make an appointment at Mr B's Reading Spa, where the team will get to know your tastes over tea and cake, then provide you with perfectly curated recommendations.

The British Pullman, A Belmond Train

The British Pullman, a grande dame of English rail, takes guests on a range of ultra-luxurious day trips across the country, including one that delivers you to Bath. The journey starts with Bellinis and a brunch featuring hyper-local ingredients, like smoked salmon from H. Forman & Son, a family-run East End institution. Tea is from Cornwall's Tregothnan, while the wines served on the return journey hail from Kent.

Each carriage is dramatically different. In Audrey, the marquetry woodwork depicts fairytale castles, while the interiors in Cygnus (originally built in the 1950s) are the work of Wes Anderson – a characteristically artful assortment of emerald fabrics, flashes of pastel-pink and swan-shaped Champagne coolers. The bathrooms even have mosaic floors, proof enough that this is worlds away from conventional train travel.

belmond.com/trains/europe/uk/belmond-british-pullman

The Cross Bath, Thermae Bath Spa

The British Pullman, A Belmond Train

Lucknam Park Hotel & Spa

The British Pullman, A Belmond Train

Lucknam Park Hotel & Spa

Topping & Company Booksellers of Bath

PEAK DISTRICT

Stately homes and centuries-old pubs

Photographs by Dan Cook

In the heart of England, spanning 555 square miles over parts of Derbyshire, Yorkshire, Staffordshire and Cheshire, lies the Peak District National Park – the first place in Britain to be awarded the title. The landscape is fittingly sublime. To the south, valleys and gorges scar the rolling limestone hills of the White Peak; in the north, Millstone grit and peat moors make the higher Dark Peak a wild and dramatic place. It's this varied terrain (which includes 1,867 miles of open access land) that makes the Peak District a hiker's paradise. But what I find most appealing is the fact that there's no shortage of characterful

pubs, meaning that almost any walk (all of which are guaranteed to come with lashings of history and the odd stately home) can begin or end by raising a glass.

When it comes to picking a trail, why not kick things off with something legendary. Thought to be the inspiration for Jane Austen's Pemberley, Chatsworth House has been home to the Dukes, Duchesses and Earls of Devonshire for 16 generations. Built by Bess of Hardwick, one of the richest, most enterprising women of the Elizabethan age, the immense 126-room stately home is crowned with 1,000 acres of landscaped parklands and

packed with a formidable art collection. It made for a regal backdrop as I meandered along the River Derwent, past fly-fishers and picnickers. In Beeley, I paused at the Devonshire Arms – where, if you believe the whispers, King Edward VII was said to have had clandestine meetings with his mistress Alice Keppel. Today, the classic village pub serves up all the staples – including a flawless burger and chips – and there's an award-winning modern brasserie for fancier fare. If you're hankering after a longer walk from Chatsworth, a circular route takes you via the Monsal Trail and the quaint village of Edensor to Bakewell, the market town that the frangipane-filled tart takes its name from.

When I headed back from Beeley through Chatsworth Park, the morning's blue sky had been replaced by cloud and the bucolic setting seemed different – still pretty, but darker and quieter. I skirted under oak branches and through a sheep-dotted orchard, wondering if this really was the route I'd taken earlier. It's amazing how the subtlest change can transform a landscape entirely.

Whitewashed, flower-festooned and welcoming revellers since 1753, the Bull's Head Inn in Foolow is a quintessential country pub, a short drive north from Chatsworth House. Food is traditional, interiors are atmospherically wonky and G&Ts taste better when sipped at an outdoor table while swapping recommendations with fellow walkers resting their weary feet in the sun. The pub stands beside a public footpath that wends across undulating fields to Eyam, making it the perfect place to savour a pint before heading to this historic hamlet. Nestled within The White Peak's limestone hills, Eyam is like something from a storybook but comes with an uncommonly harrowing past. In 1665, as travelling tailor George Viccars sat by his fire darning garments he'd carried from plague-infested London, he had no idea that the material's folds were hiding near-frozen fleas who bore the deadly illness – or that they were stirring in the warmth. This was how George unknowingly delivered the plague to Eyam. Understanding the depth of their plight and the catastrophic consequences to those around them if the sickness left the village, the community selflessly quarantined themselves. For nearly two years, no one was allowed in or out of Eyam; although this ultimately staved off the spread, two thirds of the villagers perished.

Despite its moniker as 'The Plague Village', it's hard to imagine the past suffering when you first arrive. But walk on towards the Boundary Stone (where Eyam villagers left money in vinegar-filled holes to pay for supplies left by neighbouring communities) or trek up to the Riley Graves (where, in 1666, Elizabeth Hancock buried her husband and six children, who all died within eight days of each other) and you start to see the countryside a little differently. Tumbledown cottages speak of long-lost lives, while crumbling, wildflower-enveloped stone walls are all that remain of once-flourishing farmsteads.

Our mindset (as much as the elements) can alter the way we see a landscape, and knowing what a community has experienced and the stories that have played out across a terrain shifts the way you feel. Many of the Peak District's paths have been trodden for centuries, and everyone who has ventured and lived here has left their mark. Musing on how much drama, heartbreak and wonder this bucolic landscape has witnessed made the afternoon's uphill, cross-country stomp to Bretton a little easier, my mind focused on the past rather than the increasing ache in my legs. Upon reaching this lofty hamlet, I rewarded myself with a spritz and pie at the Barrel Inn, the highest pub in Derbyshire. Given the elevation, the view come sunset is marvellous and, as I sat at a bench with a cyclist, the fields spread at our feet, she proudly told me that on cloudless days she can see five counties – although she loves the route so much that she'll ride in any weather. Back inside, history once again felt close. I like to think that centuries-old pubs (like the Barrel Inn, built in 1597) also carry echoes of all those who have revelled by their firesides. Tucking into my dinner, the chatter swirling around me, I let my mind

(right) The Bull's Head Inn, Foolow
(overleaf) Winnats Pass

Including 1,867 miles of open access land,
the Peak District's varied terrain is a hiker's paradise

drift to everyone who'd walked up here before me – and those yet to follow the trail.

Hikers seeking a casual, post-trek drinking den (i.e. 'shandy and crisps' rather than a gastropub vibe) should look to Edale's The Rambler Inn, or Ye Cheshire Cheese Inn in Castleton. Both lie on the path to Mam Tor, where paragliders take to the sky and views from the wind-softened ridge remind you just how enlivening an expansive, verdant vista can be. When the sky is clear you can see all the way to Kinder Scout, making this a great spot to pay your respects to those who paved the way for all future walkers when they took part in The Mass Trespass of Kinder Scout.

In 1932, around 400 workers – largely from the smoke-cloaked industrial cities of Sheffield and Manchester – protested the lack of public access to Derbyshire's hills by walking across the Dark Peak moorland from Hayfield to Kinder Scout, land that was then entirely privately owned. Met with opposition from gamekeepers and police, six protesters were arrested, but the resulting public outrage ultimately led to the launch of the Right to Roam movement and the Peak District's evolution into a National Park. To get better acquainted with their journey, you can follow the 8-mile route they forged, now the National Trust-managed Kinder Scout Mass Trespass Walk, a small part of which follows the hallowed, long-distance Pennine Way.

My final Peak District walk took me from Dovedale (heaving on weekends, but completely my own on a cloudy weekday) to Ilam Hall, a stately home left to the National Trust on the condition that it became a youth hostel. Seeking something serene, I crossed Dovedale's Victorian Stepping Stones, the green-gold Thorpe Cloud hill looming above me, strolled beside the caves and limestone crags lining the River Dove and claimed a deckchair in Ilam Hall's garden. To my right was a blazer-wearing gentleman sketching the shifting clouds and tussocky hills. His wife was sitting contentedly beside him, hound and abandoned book at her feet. Both were absorbed in the pastoral scene before them but, keen to get a closer look at his art, I couldn't stop myself from chatting. And that's something I've discovered while making this book: how easy it is to open up to strangers after spending time with historic sites and stunning landscapes, high on fresh air, beauty and space. As we talked about their love of the Peaks (their adopted home) and the fact I was dreading my looming departure, they told me I couldn't leave without visiting The Blind Bull, a not-so-hidden foodie treasure. So of course I made a booking there and then, aware that it's always best to trust a local – especially when it comes to superlative Peak District pubs.

DIRECTORY

Known as walking country, there are trails across the Peak District that suit every ability. For more experienced hikers, the 268-mile-long Pennine Way is a great way to explore the area and beyond (it also takes in the Yorkshire Dales and Northumberland National Park).

STAY

Buxton Crescent Hotel
Designed by the 5th Duke of Devonshire (of Chatsworth House fame) to rival the grandeur of Bath's Royal Crescent and cement Buxton's position as a premier Georgian spa town, Buxton Crescent, home to the eponymous hotel, is an architectural delight. An extensive 17-year restoration has returned the hotel to its former glory, with sleek, high-ceilinged interiors accentuating its original architectural details. Since Roman times, Buxton has stood upon some of the world's purest, mineral-rich thermal water, which can be enjoyed in the spa's thermal pool, a refurbished Victorian bath adorned with original 1920s wall tiles (the spa also comes with everything from a salt cave to a Finnish sauna).

ensanahotels.com/en/hotels/buxton-crescent
The Crescent, Buxton SK17 6BH

Wildhive Callow Hall
Cocooned within 35 acres of meadows, landscaped gardens and lupin-filled woodland at the southern edge of the National Park, this hotel celebrates the natural world – which can be admired from rooms in the fabulously decorated Hall (a revamped Victorian country house) or from one of Wildhive's treehouses. Decor across the property is the work of interior designer Isabella Worsley and stars an elegantly eccentric explosion of Pop Art prints, pressed flowers and English objects d'art. And while the interiors may be artistically vibrant, the atmosphere remains remarkably peaceful. Things feel even more sedate when suspended amongst the foliage in a one-bedroom hive or two-bedroom treehouse, where textured timber is embellished with painted floral motifs and breakfast hampers are delivered to your door. Enjoy cocktails in the Hall's library snug and dinner in the glass-walled Garden Room restaurant, or (if you're feeling active) hire a bike from the Coach House and tackle one of the walking and cycling trails that begin at Wildhive's door.

wildhive.uk
Mappleton Rd, Ashbourne DE6 2AA

EAT

The Bull's Head Inn
Adorned with vintage farming tools, this pub – just a few fields, stiles and kissing gates from Eyam – is made for walkers, with few things better preparing you for a hike than their hearty Ploughmans.

thebullsheadfoolow.co.uk
Eyam, Foolow, Hope Valley S32 5QR

The Barrel Inn
Standing at 1,300 feet above sea level, The Barrel Inn (one of just five buildings that make up the hilltop hamlet of Bretton) is Derbyshire's highest pub. Beamed ceilings, low doors, crackling log fires and flagstone floors keep things cosy and historic, while the 'Pie in the Sky' menu guarantees repeat visits.

barrelinn.co.uk
Bretton, Hope Valley S32 5QD

The Blind Bull
An inn since the 12th century, and a derelict pile of rubble for 20 years before its current gastropub incarnation, The Blind Bull may appear to be a classic village pub (with a fortnightly quiz and all) but claim a table and you'll discover that this is one for gourmands. Cocktails flow and the fare is flawless – finished with herbs and garnishes from the garden.

theblindbull.co.uk
The Blind Bull, Little Hucklow, Buxton SK17 8RT

Chatsworth Estate Farm Shop
Even with the promise of a pub at the end of a walking route, it pays to set off with supplies (for when the mid-hike munches set in). The best picnic ingredients can be gathered at Chatsworth Estate Farm Shop, where everything is either produced and made on the Estate or sourced from independent Derbyshire suppliers.

chatsworth.org/visit-chatsworth/shop-dine/farm-shop
Pilsley, Bakewell DE45 1UF

DO

Haddon Hall
Mentioned in the Domesday Book, this historic home has stayed remarkably true to its medieval origins, thanks largely to the fact that it stood empty for more than 200 years. Highlights include the 14th-century Banqueting Hall, graced with a tapestry gifted to the family by Henry VIII and the light-bathed Long Gallery with its bombee glass windows – the preferred Elizabethan background when Haddon Hall is (frequently) used as a film set.

haddonhall.co.uk
Haddon Hall, Bakewell, Derbyshire, DE45 1LA

Rail Trails
The 13-mile-long Tissington Trail follows the reclaimed London and North Western Railway line between Buxton and Ashbourne. Passing former stations and signal boxes, the scenic route is a little quieter than the hallowed Monsal Trail, another former railway route adored for its illuminated tunnels and viaducts. The Monsal Trail also has views of the Cressbrook Mill, part of the UNESCO-listed Derwent Valley Mills, a collection of 18th and 19th-century cotton mills and workers cottages that are poignant reminders of the Peak District's industrial past. This was, after all, where the Industrial Revolution began in 1771 with the opening of the water-powered Cromford Mill – although quarries have marked the landscape since the Romans first started mining here for lead.

The Blind Bull

Barrel Inn

Haddon Hall

Buxton Crescent Hotel

Wildhive Callow Hall

LAKE DISTRICT

Unwind in a wild place

Photographs by Annapurna Mellor

I don't think I'd ever been surrounded by so much green. At my feet was a bed of bracken and moss, and above me firs, pines and cedars were woven into a thick canopy. Armed with a camera (and long legs), my friend had powered ahead, so when I reached the woodland-enveloped Aira Force, a roaring, 65-foot waterfall, I stood alone in stunned silence. It was strange to think that this scene had barely changed since it inspired William Wordsworth's *The Somnambulist*, a poem about love, tragedy and the enduring power of nature.

My friend had continued uphill and, being considerably more daring than me, shimmied down a rock, draped his camera from a convenient, low-hanging branch and was bobbing contentedly in an icy black pool. We all find our own ways to commune with the natural world, and I opted for an easier method by lying with my eyes closed in the sun, allowing the water's patter to harmonise with the wind. Revived and a little sun-drunk, we walked on together, though our conversation faded as gnarled oaks and ash gave way to the heather and fern that crown the wind-blasted Gowbarrow Hill, which the 4-mile track we were following loops over. At the summit, looking out to the Pennines, the glacial lake of Ullswater

We were entirely absorbed in the landscape, the drama and intensity almost all-consuming

stretched out below us, words didn't feel necessary. We were entirely absorbed in the landscape, the drama and immensity almost all-consuming. This is what I'd come to the Lake District for: to let nature slow me down.

Covering more than 880 square miles – and comprising 14,650 archaeological sites, around 1,760 listed buildings and 23 conservation areas – the Lake District, England's largest National Park, is defined by its waterways. Bestowed with UNESCO World Heritage status in 2017, the Park's western edge is a place of extremes. It is home to Wastwater, England's deepest lake, and Scafell Pike, the country's highest peak (one of the first to climb and describe it was hillwalker Dorothy Wordsworth, William's talented sister). You can swim in Blea Tarn, which took shape during the last Ice Age, or follow the Eskdale Trail to seaside Ravenglass, a Roman naval base-turned coastal hamlet. Windermere is further south and scattered with 19 islands. As one of Britain's largest lakes, it is probably the most recognisable of the National Park's 16 named bodies of water, but it's easy to avoid the crowds by biking through the sculpture-dotted Grizedale Forest or walking up to Orrest Head. The view here is said to have inspired writer and illustrator Alfred Wainwright to pen *A Pictorial Guide to the Lakeland Fells*, a collection of seven books which have guided generations of enthusiasts since they were first published in the 1950s. As a fitting reward for his

contribution to Lakeland tourism, the area's 214 fells (uncultivated hills) are referred to as Wainwrights (Scotland's Munros have a similar origin story, taking their name from Sir Hugh Munro, the first to list the country's 283 highest peaks.)

Lured by a sense of nostalgia and the aforementioned glorious sites, the Lake District is a place I keep coming back to. I first visited as a child on a Peter Rabbit pilgrimage (this was Beatrix Potter's stomping ground) and returned for countless rainy fell walks as a university student. This time though, with slowing down my goal, I ignored the urge to explore and spent my time perfectly content beside a single lake. I settled on just one fabulous excursion (the Aira Force and Gowbarrow hike) to sate my itchy feet, yet the following days would involve doing very little indeed. This time, I'd let the Lake District work its magic by being a backdrop, and a backdrop alone.

And so, with my friend bound for London, I made the 7-mile-long Ullswater my solo base – the decision swayed, in part, by the fact that it moved Wordsworth to write *I Wandered Lonely as a Cloud*, an ode to memory and Lakeland beauty. As a literature nerd, keen to see the landscape as Wordsworth did, how could I refuse a pilgrimage? During the day, the glacial lake is crisscrossed by Ullswater Steamers, stoic wooden ferries that deliver walkers to various stops along the Ullswater Way trail. There are paddleboarders, wild swimmers (Sandwick and Mossdale Bay are particularly beautiful places for a dip) and sunset chasers with the Hallin Fell summit in their sights. But I was ensconced in Another

(left) Blea Tarn, the Langdales
(overleaf) Wastwater, the deepest lake in England

Try returning to a place you adore and picking a single walk, confident that it will be enough to re-forge a connection

Place, The Lake, a family-friendly boutique hotel on the lake's western shore. I drifted from reading in bed to strolling through the kitchen garden and rediscovered how glorious it is to do nothing but float, especially in a glass-encased pool. What surprised me most about the experience was just how easy it was to find contentment. This unwinding was out of character for me, but I'd put much-needed limits on how far I should venture and assured myself that no one would mind if I came home without a photo of Derwentwater. All I had to do was appreciate the world beyond my window.

A key part of slowing down is learning to be at ease with doing less. The urge to see it all is strong; I so often feel the need to clamber up fells or circumnavigate a lake, to fill every minute. But I not only survived my time chilling out; I thrived, returning home more rested that I'd been in months. So let this be a reminder that you don't need to tick things off the travel bucket list at breakneck speed. Instead, try returning to a place you adore and picking a single walk, confident that it will be enough to re-forge a connection. The rest of the time you can simply lounge in the sun, toast a marshmallow or bob in a lake – have an actual holiday.

(right) Eskdale, in the western Lake District

DIRECTORY

*Synonymous with 19th-century poetry and a dapper illustrated rabbit
with a penchant for blackberries, England's largest National Park (which
can easily be explored using public transport) is made for the adventurous
– and those who wish to do nothing at all.*

STAY

Another Place, The Lake

Sitting within 18 acres of National Parkland and offering views of Ullswater from almost every window, each of the 47 bedrooms in this family-friendly hotel has a unique shape and design, dictated by the original Georgian layout (with many spaces featuring vintage furniture, parquet flooring and ornate fireplaces). Book one of their six handcrafted, cedar-scented Shepherd Huts to immerse yourself in the landscape, and enjoy the king-size beds, log burners and fire pits. Daily activities including kayaking, paddleboarding and wild swimming are run from lakeside cabin the Sheep Shed, but for a calmer experience there's Swim Club, which combines a host of treatment rooms with a 65-foot, glass-enclosed pool.

another.place
Lake District National Park, Ullswater,
Watermillock CA11 0LP

Langdale Chase Hotel

With a history in hospitality reaching back to 1930, this beautifully restored, super friendly hotel on the shores of Lake Windermere is not only a great place to abscond when determined to do very little (in style) but is making waves on the culinary front. Sitting in the Dining Room over a delicious, sculptural dinner feels as if you're floating above the water; and if you don't have time to stay overnight, at least visit for afternoon tea or lunch (make sure to order the sage-dusted beetroot gnocchi if it's on the menu). There's a car on hand to deliver you to the start of walks, and in the bedrooms the watery views are all the entertainment you need.

langdalechase.co.uk
Ambleside Road, Ecclerigg, Windermere LA23 1LW

EAT

The Queen's Head

Dating to the 17th century, this is a village pub with plenty of historic charm, complete with stone walls, exposed beams and Cumbrian ales on tap. The Queen's Head uses a range of ingredients grown in the Askham Kitchen Garden (part of Askham Hall, which is also home to the Michelin-starred Allium restaurant), while others are foraged or sourced from Lakeland farmers.

queensheadaskham.co.uk
Askham, Penrith CA10 2PF

The Victorian Glasshouse

Offering fabulous fell views and serving cocktails and stone-baked pizzas made with Cumbrian ingredients, The Victorian Glasshouse is surrounded by flourishing gardens which have been planted with native bees and butterflies in mind. This is one of the three restaurants at Another Place, The Lake – head to swish Rampsbeck for a more formal experience.

another.place/food-drink/restaurants/the-glasshouse
Lake District National Park, Another Place The Lake,
Ullswater, Watermillock CA11 0LP

The Bakery at No. 4, Kendal

Stock up on treats from The Bakery at No. 4. The menu is ever-changing, with the team building their bakes around what is local and in season (resulting in creations like the cheddar, potato, onion and chorizo jam roll), so repeat visits are highly recommended.

bakery4.co.uk
40 Woolpack Yard, Kendal LA9 4NG

DO

My trip to the Lake District deliberately involved doing very little. However, if you are after a more active escape, here are some suggestions.

Follow Wordsworth's footsteps

To see the landscape as William Wordsworth did, set out from Dove Cottage in Grasmere (the house he shared with his sister and family, now a museum) and walk to Rydal. You'll pass Dora's Field, which is blanketed in daffodils every spring, the first bulbs planted by Worthsworth as a moving memorial to his daughter, Dora.

Hill Top

Formerly Beatrix Potter's holiday retreat and eventual home, this 17th-century Lakeland farmhouse has been preserved as she left it. The space is full of Potter's diaries, photographs and sketches, and the garden still thrives. An avid farmer and conservationist, Potter left almost all her property (4,000 acres and 14 farms) to the National Trust, who are now the Lake District's chief landowners.

nationaltrust.org.uk/visit/lake-district/hill-top
near Sawrey, Ambleside LA22 0LF

Old Man of Coniston

Once alive with slate and copper mines, the Old Man of Coniston (one of the Lake District's higher fells, historically used as a training ground for Everest climbers) takes hours to climb, but the summit view is astounding, as are the glacier-clear pools you pass on the way up.

Aira Force

This phenomenal waterfall, hidden away beside Ullswater (on land managed by the National Trust), is found near the start of the circular, 4.5-mile-long Gowbarrow Trail.

near Watermillock, Penrith, Cumbria, CA11 0JS

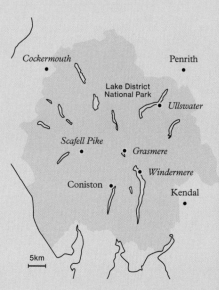

Langdale Chase

Langdale Chase

The Queen's Head

Dove Cottage

Wastwater

Another Place, The Lake

HADRIAN'S WALL

Walk at the edge of an ancient empire

Photographs by Joel Clifton

Northumberland is a county suited to autumn, the moorland's velvety hues and turning leaves made all the more dramatic by the swirling mist and drizzle. There is no better stage for the lichen-covered stone colossus that is Hadrian's Wall, one of England's ancient architectural marvels. Spanning the breadth of the country from Newcastle to Cumbria, forts like Housesteads, Vindolanda, Birdoswald and Chesters line what remains of this mighty construction – rousing reminders of the past glories of the Roman Empire.

One of the most popular ways of exploring the Wall is to hike along the 84-mile-long National Trail named in its honour – the ultimate mode of slow travel. Set out and you'll be walking with history – something that hit home for me when I hiked through Sycamore Gap, which stands high above the glacial Crag Lough. Here, the autumn weather proved temperamental, but even though the lake was obscured by cloud and the sycamore sadly felled, the scene was still enthralling. The Wall rose from the earth, draping itself over the ridgeline, following the terrain's natural dips and folds. How they built this vast structure thousands of years ago boggles the mind. Ramble along any drystone wall in rural England and you'll be

This monument to Imperial Rome is so evocative that if you close your eyes, you can practically hear the tread of booted feet

reminded of how far back into history this country's past stretches. But travel along the Wall, which is scattered with the remains of temples, towers and bathhouses, and you'll begin to understand what ancient truly means.

Hadrian had the benefit and the burden of coming to power when the Roman Empire was at the peak of its strength and territorial reach. And he was well-suited to the task, recognising (unlike his predecessors) that Rome needed stability far more than it did endless battles fought in the pursuit of ever-expanding borders. As with any successful Roman ruler, good relations with the military were vital, and Hadrian's appreciation of this served him well. Although he was known for his strict discipline, Hadrian also rewarded the deserving among his ranks and bolstered loyalty by living off the same rations as his soldiers on the various marches he led.

Despite the softness of the English mizzle and the gently curving landscape, this distant edge of Roman Britannia was a harsh environment. Arriving here in AD 43, Roman troops initially maintained an uneasy peace with the Brigantes in the north, who were led by their wily queen Cartimandua. But after several revolts by the Brigantes and other British tribes, diplomacy was abandoned in favour of occupation, culminating in the Wall's construction from AD 122. Its presence served multiple purposes: as a symbol of the Roman Empire's strength and as a bulwark against the fierce northern tribes, preventing them from disrupting the growing prosperity of Romanised southern Britannia.

At one time more than 13 feet high (but still formidable in its ruinous state), it's tempting to dwell purely on the Wall's military significance. But it's fascinating to discover that the structure also contained 16 forts that housed soldiers and their families along with all the other apparatus of Roman life – including temples, stables and famously luxurious plumbing. There were even traders and merchants who linked these remote communities to the economy of the wider Empire. A letter recovered at Vindolanda, one such fort, requests a large delivery of olives – customary fare for Romans, you might think, but pretty exotic by early British culinary standards.

The Wall was also shaped by the Roman preoccupation with all things spiritual, speaking to both the ethnic diversity of the Roman army's recruits and the empire's habit of enfolding local customs into its own. The Temple of Mithras, at the base of an immense grassy mound (the unassuming remains of Carrawburgh Fort), was built to worship the eponymous god from the far eastern reaches of the empire. Alone at this site, surrounded by the worn recreations of the temple's alter and statues, I could sense the reverence and awe of centuries past. While much of Mithraism is shrouded in mystery, soldiers may have been drawn to this cult because of the value it placed on courage and military skill.

(left) A statue at Vindolanda

The Wall rose from the earth, draping itself over the ridgeline, following the terrain's natural dips and folds

Walk on for five miles from the temple and you'll reach Housesteads, Britain's most complete Roman fort, which once housed more than 800 soldiers. Each one of the forts – now haunting, open-air ruins – is unique, not just because of what they contain (be it a temple, hospital or fascinating example of early underfloor heating) but because of the feelings they evoke. Housesteads, in particular, is a place of time slips, and an hour here disappeared without me noticing. As I looked out from the remains of a watchtower at the end of a thick length of Wall that ran down the valley, it was clear to me that this isn't solely a space for history buffs. The way these ruins are entwined with the landscape is part of the allure. You start to imagine what once stood here, the gates, houses and towers that have been devoured by the elements. The structures themselves are astounding, but so is the fact that nature reclaims all.

Those entranced by the Wall have one man in particular to thank for its preservation: John Clayton. After inheriting his family's estate at Chesters in 1832, Clayton (who had long been fascinated by the Romans) began excavating a curious mound by the river, uncovering a flight of stairs that led to a ruined building. Recognising

the tell-tale signs of a Roman bathhouse – a heating system, furnace soot and the pinkish cement of a bath – he knew he'd come across something special. Clayton would go on to spend his fortune excavating Chesters and purchasing other sites along the Wall to preserve them. He also persuaded fellow landowners to stop blowing up sections that were interfering with farming or repurposing the stone, which had become a hardy building material all those centuries later. Today, organisations such as the Vindolanda Charitable Trust also work to ensure the Wall's survival as a piece of living history.

Standing by a rain-lashed portion of the Wall near Birdoswald in Cumbria, I wondered what the Roman soldiers stationed here thought of this landscape, so wildly green and grey, and worlds away from vivid, sunbaked Italian climes. This monument to Imperial Rome is so evocative that if you close your eyes, you can practically hear the tread of booted feet and the whistle of stiff northern winds setting armour and weaponry clanking. Slicing its way across the landscape, Hadrian's Wall is a singular reminder of our connection to far-flung lands and times, a steadfast stony link to the past. I felt reassuringly small in its presence.

(right) A section of the Wall near Sycamore Gap

DIRECTORY

Stretching for 73 miles from Wallsend in Newcastle-upon-Tyne to Bowness-on-Solway near Carlisle, Hadrian's Wall (built a little more than 1,900 years ago) is part of the Frontiers of the Roman Empire World Heritage Site. To get acquainted with it, hike the multi-day Hadrian's Wall Path or spend time with a few of its icons.

STAY

Lord Crewe Arms

This history-packed, dog-friendly hotel, found in the heart of honey-hued Blanchland, is as atmospheric as they come. Once the abbot's lodge of a 12th-century priory, many of the original building's architectural details remain, from arched stone doorways to flagstone floors. The Lord Crewe hosts a range of seasonal activities including stargazing (Northumberland National Park has been a Dark Sky Park since 2013). Year round you can enjoy afternoon tea by the fire in the banqueting hall, watched over by armour and shields. It's also worth whiling away an evening in the Crypt Bar, a vaulted chamber illuminated by candlelight, before you head upstairs to feast in the rustic Bishop's Dining Room.

lordcrewearmsblanchland.co.uk
The Square, Blanchland, Consett DH8 9SP

EAT

Grant's Bakery

Once the northernmost town in the Roman Empire, Corbridge now comes with buckets of historical charm. Visit the Corbridge Hoard, wander the town's cobbled, cafe-dotted streets and then pop into Grant's Bakery to stock up on all the baked treats needed to fuel you on a fort-filled hike (their Florentines are especially good).

grantsbakery.co.uk
1 Market Pl, Corbridge NE45 5AW

Restaurant Hjem

To break up your adventure with a little lavishness, book a table at this Michelin-starred restaurant. The creation of Swedish chef Alex Nietosvuori and his partner, Northumberland-born restaurant manager Ally Thompson, Hjem (which translates as home) combines Scandinavian traditions with outstanding English ingredients. The results are as delicious as you'd imagine.

restauranthjem.co.uk
The Hadrian Hotel, Front St, Wall, Hexham NE46 4EE

The Rat Inn

This 18th-century pub in the tiny hamlet of Anick is a great place to head for a leisurely Sunday roast. Chamberpots (now art) hang from the ceiling, a carriage wheel has been converted into a chandelier and you'll likely spy a sheep or two grazing on the neighbouring village green.

theratinn.com
Anick, Hexham NE46 4LN

Feathers Inn

Treasured by foodies, the family-run Feathers Inn has been crowned The Good Pub Guide's County Dining Pub of The Year for 16 years and counting – just one of the slew of awards the pub has received. It also has a seasonal pop-up pizzeria and patisserie.

thefeathers.net
Hedley on the Hill, Stocksfield NE43 7SW

DO

Birdoswald Roman Fort

The longest continuous stretch of the Wall is found at Birdoswald. Follow it in either direction and you'll be amazed by how this ancient moment is part of everyday life, merging with drystone walls, lining roads and marking the boundaries of fields.

Gilsland, Brampton CA8 7DD

Chesters Roman Fort and Museum

Unearthed by John Clayton, Chesters is Britain's most complete Roman cavalry fort and home to the remains of an ancient bathhouse, set beside the River North Tyne. View a range of Clayton's finds in the on-site museum.

Chollerford, Hexham NE46 4EU

Vindolanda and the Roman Army Museum

In use for more than 400 years, Vindolanda Fort pre-dates the Wall and was demolished and rebuilt nine times during its existence. Plan your visit right and you'll see archaeologists and volunteers at work on this active excavation site.

vindolanda.com
Hexham NE47 7JN

Housesteads Roman Fort

Crowning the Whin Sill escarpment, the astoundingly well-preserved Housesteads features the remains of barracks and watchtowers, a hospital and even one of England's oldest communal toilets. Housesteads is a 5-mile walk from the Temple of Mithras, but head west and you'll reach Sycamore Gap. Although the tree has been felled (there are hopes it will re-grow from the stump), the spot remains stunning, and standing in the saddle you can understand why this site was chosen as the best place to keep an eye on the horizon.

near Hexham, Northumberland NE47 6NN

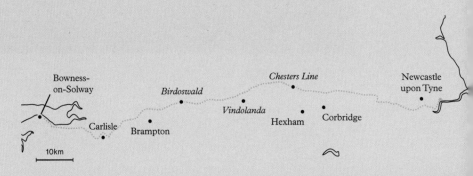

Lord Crewe Arms

The Rat Inn

Vindolanda Roman Fort

Housesteads Roman Fort

SCOTLAND

EDINBURGH

A city where nature sits centre-stage

Photographs by Daisy Wingate-Saul

The best way to experience Edinburgh (or any city for that matter), is to strike up a conversation with someone who calls it home. They'll know where the treasures lie and where to head when craving gardens and salt air. And if the person you're talking to happens to be a sustainability-focused travel writer or an artistically inclined florist, then that's even better. For this is a metropolis built around volcanoes and lochs, a place where escaping into nature (a vital ingredient when it comes to slow travel) is part of everyday life. Edinburgh is awash with wild spaces – serene corners that don't just provide respite from the city's hustle but blur the boundaries between the urban and untamed. Here you can wander among heather, scramble up hillsides and swim in the sea. So, it's little wonder that locals are proud (and appreciative) of all that's on offer.

My initial introduction to nature-packed Edinburgh came from Fiona Inglis, who helms Pyrus, a botanical studio that is behind several works and collaborative projects across the city – although she grows her blooms in a Victorian walled garden (complete with a rose tunnel, woodland and beehives) in neighbouring East Lothian. Fiona co-founded Pyrus with Natalya Ayers (who has

*This is a metropolis built around mountains,
volcanoes and lochs, a place where escaping
into nature is part of everyday life*

since moved to the Italian mountains) and continues to work almost exclusively with unusual Scottish native and heritage varieties – from wild gorse and heather to foxgloves and gnarly Scots pine roots – and foraging remains an important part of her practice. One of her most striking creations was an installation for the National Galleries of Scotland's 2016 Impressionists exhibition, where she wrapped the National's external pillars in poppies, cornflowers and blossoms. The piece did more than evoke a poppy field; it drew attention to Edinburgh's unique relationship with the natural world. Because in this city, you don't need to travel far to find yourself somewhere green.

'Living in Edinburgh is special,' Fiona begins. 'Its geography is quite singular. We're flanked by sea, hills, farms and woodland, with an extinct volcano in the heart of the city. You can't escape nature here, and that proximity to the elements influences everything in daily life... the seasons are so evident. In early spring, the gorse blooms deliver a gentle coconut scent over the hills; in late spring, the trees in the Meadows burst into clouds of pink blossom. It's inevitable that this is reflected in the work at Pyrus. The crags and skyline of Arthur's Seat always remind me how beautiful our landscape is and fuel my love of texture.'

Fiona finds her solace on the mile-long Portobello Beach, an expanse of golden sand backdropped

by the North Sea, and she always makes time for the Royal Botanic Garden, Calton Hill and the Meadows. 'I'm so lucky to call Edinburgh home. I feel very spoiled,' she says. 'It's so important to have accessible green spaces in the city, to clear your mind and reset, especially in this fast-paced age. It is easy to lose sight of the bigger picture without it.'

I frequently find myself in Edinburgh, drawn to the creative buzz (this is a UNESCO City of Literature after all) as much as its wilder elements. It's a city I first fell for when embracing my inner bohemian during the annual Fringe Festival – a month-long performing arts festival that kicked off in 1947. I've walked Arthur's Seat, passing St Margaret's Lock and the 600-year-old ruins of Saint Anthony's Chapel on my clamber up this extinct volcano, the city sprawled at my feet from the summit. I've seen the wildflower meadow at the Johnston Terrace Garden in the shadow of Edinburgh Castle, lazed with a book in the Princes Street Garden and stood atop the volcanic Carlton Hill, with its neoclassical monuments and an observatory, a site that perfectly captures that singular union of natural and built environments.

On my most recent trip for this book I found a patch of wilderness I hadn't explored before: the tranquil Water of Leith. Travelling through the heart of Edinburgh, this walkway is a designated Urban Wildlife Site, where brown trout, cormorants, otters and Antony Gormley's sculptures thrive among plants like sweet cicely and water mint. One of the walk's most picturesque stretches

(previous) Dean Village, formerly a 12th-century milling community and now a symbol of the city's industrial past
(left) Tending the Pyrus gardens

171

passes through Dean Village, which first emerged as a milling community in the 12th century and is now a striking symbol of the city's industrial past. This jumble of stone buildings sits right beside the water (a perfect mirror on calm, sunny days) and is particularly resplendent when the houses catch the early evening light. Standing on the arched architectural gem that is Dean Bridge, which links Dean Village to Edinburgh's New Town, it appears as though the centuries-old terraces are cradled by the riverside trees, creating the illusion of a city growing from a forest.

I'd heard about the Water of Leith from Jack Cairney, who founded the magazine and website *Hidden Scotland* with his partner Karla Hall to promote his country's less-travelled roads. Jack is acutely aware of Edinburgh's green appeal, and just how good that can be for the soul, something he was reminded of while working on Hidden Scotland's *The Best of* guide to the city. When I ask why he writes about Edinburgh (and Scotland) his answer is simple: 'While distant lands fascinate us, there's a unique allure in the familiar landscapes and stories of our own nation.'

There are several green spaces that stand out to Jack. The 72-acre Royal Botanic Garden in Stockbridge is a horticultural wonder, and Dunbar's Close in the Old Town a lesser-known treasure. 'It's a peaceful spot with its handsome trees and neat garden beds, offering a quiet escape right off the bustling Royal Mile,' he describes. 'For something a bit more secluded, Dr Neil's Garden in the Southside is a delight. Created by doctors Andrew and Nancy Neil, this garden by Duddingston Loch blends evergreens, heathers and seasonal flowers, creating a serene oasis away from the city's hustle.'

Jack explains that many of these places exist because early civil planners made the bold decision to incorporate Edinburgh's natural geography into the urban landscape. But they aren't the city's only charms. 'The Scottish capital, with its taverns, tenements, steep cobbled streets and ancient hills, topped by a mighty, cliff-perched castle, is like something from a gilt-edged storybook,' Jack observes. 'Yet it's also a living, sleepless metropolis, brimming with energy, creativity and a serious culinary and creative pedigree. The contrast between the historic Royal Mile and the vibrant festivals, quality galleries, restaurants and pubs showcases a city that is both a museum piece and a dynamic, contemporary hub.' Although it's easy to sometimes forget while ambling along quiet waterways, Edinburgh is a city defined as much by its architecture and cultural scene as the bounty of nature on display. But I'm starting to think that these two worlds (the built and the wild) feel particularly dazzling here because of the contrast. It's so special being able to explore near-empty rivers, meadows and hills when restaurants and museums are a mere stone's throw away – and castles seem particularly charming when framed by greenery.

Talking to Jack and Fiona changed the way I saw the city. I thought I understood its allure, but immersing myself in its peaks and waterways (guided by those who know them well), and experiencing just how entwined the urban and natural really are, has made me adore Edinburgh and its green spaces all the more.

(right) The Pyrus gardens

DIRECTORY

Edinburgh is easy to reach by train – try the Caledonian Sleeper if you're travelling from London and fancy an overnight journey.

STAY

Gleneagles Townhouse
Blending original Georgian features with soothing pastel shades, flashes of marble and huge contemporary artworks, this bank-turned-hotel is one for design-devotees. Bedrooms tip their debonaire hats to the past and come with king-size beds, ornate cornicing and lashings of art. In the spa, facilities include a gym, cryotherapy chamber and infrared saunas, while the changing rooms are tucked within the former bank vaults. The Art Deco tree-topped bar is the hotel's centrepiece, positioned beneath a glass dome (another architectural detail left over from the building's time as a bank).
gleneagles.com/townhouse
39 St Andrew Square, Edinburgh EH2 2AD

EAT

The Little Chartroom
This inviting, family-run restaurant near the Water of Leith was established by chef Roberta Hall-McCarron and her husband Shaun McCarron, who runs the front of house. Renowned for its contemporary Scottish cuisine and focus on locally sourced ingredients, each dish served in their three or five course menus is a vibrant and innovative work of art.
thelittlechartroom.com
14 Bonnington Rd, Edinburgh EH6 5JD

Timberyard
Set inside a revamped 19th-century warehouse originally built to store costumes and props, a meal at Timberyard is bound to involve some memorable culinary theatrics. The Radford family's creativity with exceptional ingredients makes them more than deserving of their Michelin star. The entire space is elegantly pared-back and their private room, The Shed, can be hired for special gatherings.
timberyard.co
10 Lady Lawson St, Edinburgh, EH3 9DS

The Spence at Gleneagles
'Spence' is the Scottish word for larder, so naturally Head Chef Johny Wright's menu is an ode to the country's rich culinary heritage. There are juicy Mull scallops, tender rump fillet from the Tweed Valley and sweet langoustines that complement the interior's peachy hues. Be sure to save room for the dessert trolley, a fitting finale.
gleneagles.com/townhouse
39 St Andrew Square, Edinburgh EH2 2AD

DO

Bookshops
Crowned a UNESCO City of Literature, Edinburgh is rich in bookish charm and has been home to Walter Scott, Arthur Conan Doyle, Robert Louis Stevenson, J. M. Barrie, Muriel Spark and many more besides. You can connect with these icons in places like Topping & Company Booksellers (which hosts regular talks and events), Lighthouse Bookshop (where the team are passionate about supporting emerging writers), Portobello Bookshop (ideal for beach-going bookworms) and Golden Hare Books (which might just have the country's best reading recommendations).

The Scottish National Gallery of Modern Art
The Scottish National Gallery of Modern Art features two distinctive, art-filled buildings, Modern One and Modern Two, which are enveloped by an outdoor sculpture park, and can be reached from the Water of Leith. Between the galleries are thriving yet semi-secret allotment gardens famed for their apples – pockets of calm amidst the city's thrum.
nationalgalleries.org/visit/scottish-national-gallery-
*   modern-art*
73 & 75 Belford Rd, Edinburgh, EH4 3DR

Arthur's Seat
An extinct volcano looming 823 feet above sea level, boasting superlative views over the city (allow a couple of hours to walk to the top and back).

Dunbar's Close
It's easy to miss this peaceful garden beside the Royal Mile, marked with just a modest plaque. Named after 18th-century writer David Dunbar, who once owned the neighbouring tenements, it is a serene oasis away from the bustle.
137 Canongate, Edinburgh EH8 8BW

The Royal Botanic Garden
One of the world's leading botanic gardens with a rich collection of plants. Check their programme of events for tours and talks, or simply wander among the Living Collection (including plants over 350 years old).
rbge.org.uk
Edinburgh EH3 5NZ

Dr Neil's Garden
This secluded haven beside Duddington Loch is the work of doctors Andrew and Nancy Neil, who understood the restorative benefits of being outdoors and encouraged their patients to help cultivate the land on the north side of Arthur's Seat. Today, it feels like a secret garden, filled with winding paths and wildlife.
drneilsgarden.co.uk
5 Old Church Ln, Duddingston, Edinburgh EH15 3PX

Gleneagles Townhouse

The Spence at Gleneagles

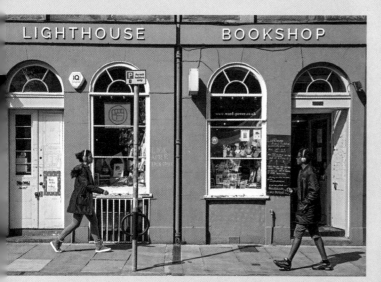

Lighthouse Bookshop

Arthur's Seat

The Spence at Gleneagles

Dr Neil's Garden

Timberyard

Princess Street Gardens

Timberyard

The Little Chartroom

Dunbar's Close

The Little Chartroom

Royal Botanic Gardens

CAIRNGORMS

Read the mountains

Photographs by Orlando Gili

Nan Shepherd was ahead of her time. Born just outside Aberdeen in 1893, she was a writer, poet and teacher who, through her seminal book, *The Living Mountain*, revealed just how wondrous and necessary time immersed in the natural world can be. Written in the 1940s (but hidden in a drawer for more than 30 years), the book is an ode to the Cairngorms, the UK's largest National Park: a staggering mass of granite peaks (many over 13,000 feet high) that were once higher than the Alps. Shepherd championed moving slowly; she took time with her surrounds, appreciating the smells, shapes and elements,

rather than racing to a summit. Well before it was in vogue, Shepherd was aware of the connection between an external landscape and our inner workings; how nature not only shapes our thinking, but our understanding of who we are.

Shepherd did most of her work from a red-roofed croft in the town of Braemar, a place where she could live and breathe the Cairngorms. When I devoured her nature writing as a student in Australia, the landscapes she described – a mass of juniper, heather and birch, towering Munros and brutal winters (the Cairngorms' high mountains are the coldest place in Britain) – seemed far-flung

Shepherd believed that we needed to use all our senses to experience the Cairngorms

and improbably wild. When I finally visited the region, more than a decade later, I'd come to indulge in art and luxury at The Fife Arms hotel, so imagine my surprise when, upon checking in, I learned that her croft was a mere half-hour walk uphill. From that moment on, my trip changed. I wanted to see these mountains as Shepherd did.

Even before Shepherd arrived, Braemar was a place of storytellers. Robert Louis Stevenson had a cottage in town where he wrote parts of *Treasure Island*, and Lord Byron spent some of his childhood in Deeside. His Highlands poetry includes *Dark Lochnagar*, and climbing this eponymous Munro today is a great way to appreciate the Cairngorms' scale and understand how remote this wilderness truly is. Although Sir Walter Scott never ventured this far north, he helped bring tourism to the Highlands through the popularity of his *Waverley* novels (which captured the romance of the Jacobite period) and his fascination, like Shepherd, with the ways nature could help heal the mind.

This literary history was imparted to me by Fife guide Shona Armstrong. A member of the Mountain Rescue team (an absolute lifeline among these beautiful but punishing peaks), Shona joined The Fife Arms after retiring as the town's GP, but it was the inaugural Braemar Literary Festival in 2022 that inspired her to start nature-centric literary tours for the hotel, many of which end at Shepherd's croft.

(overleaf) Guide Léopold Amory;
Early-morning view from Creag Choinnich

Shona also drew my attention to Shepherd's playfulness and how having a fondness for wildness and solitude doesn't always result in a serious persona. Reading from her beloved first edition of *The Living Mountain* (a family heirloom), Shona revealed one of Shepherd's simple, almost childlike ways of seeing a landscape anew – a technique we can still employ to notice the little things that are frequently overlooked: 'Lay the head down, or better still, face away from what you look at, and bend with straddled legs till you see your world upside down. How new it has become! From the close-by sprigs of heather to the most distant fold of the land, each detail stands erect in its own validity.'

The following frosty morning, I joined Shona's niece Annie on a walk and swim in the National Park. Operating custom walking, swimming and foraging adventures for Fife guests, Annie feels a connection to Shepherd (who taught her grandmother at Aberdeen College of Education) and shares her approach to these Munros, taking her time to get to know them, to revel in exploration and discovery rather than dashing to the top. We stopped along our hike to touch frozen bog myrtle and juniper, its sweet scent released as I rolled a dried berry in my hand, and I started to embrace the mystical. We were surrounded by mountain birch, which Annie likes to think is the domain of Ghillie Dhu – a fairy who is happy for children to play in his birch forests, but is wary of adults, given their fondness of cutting down trees. If you ever stumble in the woods, or are hit by a branch, that's his doing. Keen to see this terrain as a place

of stories and myth, I found myself listening more intently, hyper-aware of my senses (in a spirited attempt to hear the rustle of fairy footsteps). Shepherd believed that we needed to use all our senses to experience the Cairngorms, from sight, which granted her entry to 'the world of light, of colour, of shape, of shadow', to sound, something that is beautiful even in its absence: 'For the ear, the most vital thing that can be listened to here is silence. To bend the ear to silence is to discover how seldom it is there. Always something moves.'

Our day had begun hours earlier with a traipse through thick mist, the icy ground crackling under my feet, to Pulladh, a natural pool on the River Dee. Looking at the rippling water, I understood what Shepherd meant when she described a loch as being 'frost-cold to the fingers'. Even Annie, who has been exploring these waterways since she was two, took a moment to summon up the courage to swim. No matter how much experience you have with cold water, it's normal to lose that childlike desire to simply jump in. But it's exhilarating when you finally do.

On my final morning, I set out from The Fife Arms under cover of darkness, walking through dense Scots Pine to Creag Choinnich (Gaelic for 'mossy hill'). My heart pounded on the ascent, the sound of my breathing occasionally drowned out by the call of rutting stags, easily mistaken for disgruntled cows. I trudged uphill in silence, still

groggy from sleep, yet at the summit, all my early morning moodiness slipped away. Above me, the sky was glowing, the sunrise a mesmeric mix of tangerine and blush that lit up the frost-covered heather like snow. Returning to town, my feet light and my mind clear, I passed a kilted man at the hill's base, a leather suitcase in his hand. He was off to practise his bagpipes in the forest, a personal morning ritual – a reminder that there is no one way to embrace the natural world.

What astounds me most about the Cairngorms is just how much exists in a relatively small space. You could hike for days over the park's 55 Munros (four of which are the UK's highest), or simply sit by the Dee with your back against the sun-warmed stone of an old croft and let the scene wash over you. Either way, the next time you set out everything will seem completely transformed, new details emerging with every adventure. Even if you were to return to the same spot, there are subtle changes at play: the movement of a cloud or herd of deer, the slow shifting of the seasons. This all alters what we see and feel, our perception more in sync with nature's rhythms than we might realise. As Shepherd writes: 'One never quite knows the mountain, nor oneself in relation to it. However often I walk on them, these hills hold astonishments for me. There is no getting accustomed to them.'

(right) Annie Armstrong, who runs walking, swimming and foraging adventures for guests of The Fife Arms

DIRECTORY

If you drive up from Edinburgh, you'll fall in love with the Cairngorms the moment you enter Glenshee (Scotland's largest ski area). Even when it's not blanketed in snow, this deer-dotted expanse sets the Highland mood perfectly. But to swoon over the Cairngorms from afar, dive into Nan Shepherd's books and poetry.

STAY

The Fife Arms

Opened by the duo behind Hauser & Wirth global gallery, this boutique five-star hotel is the beating heart of Braemar and an art-filled oasis (there are around 16,000 pieces in its collection). A Pieter Brueghel the Younger hangs in the Clunie Dining Room, contrasted by a room-sized mural from Argentinian artist Guillermo Kuitca, its sharp angles and dark hues a homage to the River Dee. There are photos from Man Ray, a painted ceiling in the drawing room that's part abstract topographic map, part homage to Cairngorms crystal, an antique chimneypiece inspired by the poetry of Robert Burns and an original drawing by Queen Victoria.

The Fife is devoted to showcasing the wonders of the Cairngorms, with every room designed to reflect local nature, poetry and personalities. There are activities aplenty, from drawing in nature to fishing and foraging, and a team of dapper ghillies are on hand to curate experiences. But there are plenty of reasons to stay in, too – like Elsa's cocktail bar, named for Surrealist fashion designer Elsa Schiaparelli, a regular visitor to nearby Braemar Castle.

thefifearms.com
Mar Rd, Braemar, Ballater AB35 5YN

EAT

Fish Shop

This exceptional restaurant and fishmonger is all about sustainability. The abstract bar is made from recycled beer and wine bottles while tables are crafted from recycled yoghurt pots. The wine list features tipples exclusively from the Northern Hemisphere (keeping the air miles low) and the team only use sustainable suppliers, many of whom are found using the age-old method of 'knowing someone who knows someone'. The Cape Wrath oysters are perfect, and the British bluefin tuna crumpet is unforgettable.

fishshopballater.co.uk
3 Netherley Place, Ballater, AB35 5QE

The Flying Stag

Part of The Fife Arms, The Flying Stag is an oft-packed pub (watched over by a winged, taxidermied stag) that specialises in classic Scottish fare and ales. An entire wall is lined with portraits of locals (how else do you prove you're a village pub?), and an alcove contains a cabinet of curiosities filled with an assortment of stuffed animals. The pub is a hop and skip from the sumptuously decorated Bertie's Whisky Bar, for those who want to celebrate in style.

thefifearms.com/eat-drink/flying-stag
Mar Rd, Braemar, Ballater AB35 5YN

DO

Balmoral Castle & Estate

Balmoral Castle and Estate was purchased by Queen Victoria in 1852, after she fell in love with the area while staying nearby with her physician. She promptly set about rebuilding the shooting lodge, turning it into the Gothic, German-style castle that the Royal Family still visit every summer. Queen Victoria did a huge amount to promote Highlands tourism, writing extensive diaries during her time at Balmoral. She and Albert often travelled incognito, by pony or foot, staying at simple inns and cottages, and made their way up and over some of the UK's highest Munros. You can visit the Balmoral Castle grounds, free of charge, on certain days in autumn and winter.

balmoralcastle.com
Balmoral Estates, Ballater AB35 5TB

Mar Lodge Estate

Covering more than 29,000 hectares and managed by the National Trust for Scotland, this is Britain's largest National Nature Reserve. Thanks to a rewilding scheme that has been operating for more than 30 years, and efforts to keep the deer population under control, young rowen, alder and aspen trees thrive (a rare sight in Scotland). One of the most iconic Mar Lodge sites is the Devil's Punch Bowl at Linn of Quoich. During the first Jacobite rebellion, supporters swore allegiance to the Stuart cause by drinking a mixture of whisky and honey from a hole in the rock, which the river has carved out further over the ensuing 300 years.

nts.org.uk/visit/places/mar-lodge-estate
Braemar, Ballater AB35 5YJ

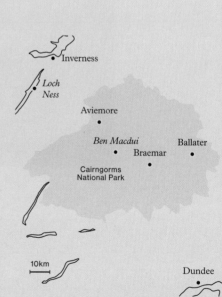

Inverness

Loch Ness

Aviemore

Ben Macdui
Braemar
Ballater

Cairngorms National Park

10km

Dundee

The Fife Arms

The Fife Arms

Mar Lodge Estate

The Flying Stag

The Fife Arms

Fish Shop

LOCH LOMOND & THE TROSSACHS

Learn to embrace wild weather

Photographs by Orlando Gili

At times, slowing down isn't a choice but a necessity, something demanded by fickle weather gods who have decided to unleash an abundance of rain rather than the sun typically demanded by the season. And once the heavens open, all you can do is move at a pace that the mud and mizzle allow. The wind might keep you from walking as far or climbing as high (the classic Scottish pursuit of 'Munro bagging' off the menu), but there's beauty in bleak weather. Stormy skies add character, softening a landscape and drawing out the details you might otherwise overlook. Clouds play with perspective and

illuminate the minutiae. Even on the most inhospitable days, there will be something that sets your spirits soaring – so long as you're still game enough to venture out.

Wet weather forced me to slow down on a recent sojourn to Loch Lomond and the Trossachs National Park, an oasis of forests, waterfalls and craggy, gale-battered peaks (even when cloaked in cloud). I'd come to climb a handful of its 21 Munros and spend time by its lochs, after a Glaswegian friend assured me that the gin-clear Loch Katrine was resplendent on a blue-sky day (and best viewed from atop Ben A'an hill),

Vistas don't need to be sun-kissed and expansive to be sublime

while Loch Chon is said to have a resident kelpie (shape-shifting spirit). But the gusty conditions meant that I spent most of my time beside the 22-mile-long Loch Lomond – Britain's largest freshwater loch, by surface area at least. Bisected by the Highland Boundary Fault (which marks the shift from Scotland's Lowlands to its Highlands), it is scattered with around 30 islands, and lined with walking paths, time-forgotten towns and rolling mountains that appear more dramatic the further north you travel. But far from dampening the landscape, the rain added to the romance, with the autumnal shades contrasted by a deep, thundery sky.

Loch Lomond is also synonymous with Robert MacGregor (better known as Rob Roy), a red-haired, Robin Hood-esque figure romanticised eternally by Sir Walter Scott. After starting out as a livestock trader in the late 1700s, he set about robbing and fighting on behalf of his clan (who were often ill-treated by landlords) and did quite well for himself in the process. Tales of his bravery and swordsmanship quickly became lore across the Lowlands, and for years he used lochside caves and crevices as his hideouts, before finally turning himself over to the authorities in exchange for a short sentence and quieter life. It's much easier to imagine Rob Roy's daring-do when the clouds are low, obscuring the blue-black Loch Lomond. There is a sense of mysticism and intrigue; as you look out across the whipped-up water, it's easy to understand why the Scots

(left) Aubrey and Iwen, fellow walkers

idolised the bold and dreamt up stories of selkies (seals that could shed their skin and take on human form), usually tied to tales of lost loves. In settings this majestic, there is often more than one legend at play.

Things felt just as magical while climbing Conic Hill above the town of Balmaha, part of the 95-mile-long West Highland Way that winds along the loch. On a clear day, you can see all the way to Ben Lomond, Scotland's most southerly Munro. But as I edged closer to the summit with the roar of the wind all-consuming, all I could make out were a handful of islands, hidden every now and then by the mist that tumbled over the surrounding hills. Even with most of the scene lost in a sea of white, it was enough to hint at Loch Lomond's staggering scale.

As I retraced my steps back down to Balmaha and the warmth of its pub, I kept getting caught up in conversations with fellow trampers. There's a sense of camaraderie among those brave enough to battle puddles and heights, perfectly content in the knowledge that a view is unlikely to be waiting. You always swap more than a 'hello'; you want to know what has brought people out in such punishing weather (beyond the simple joy of a walk) and share the loveliness spotted en route – raindrops on foliage or streams that only flow when it buckets. Everyone I passed seemed blissfully aware that vistas don't need to be sun-kissed and expansive to be sublime.

The following day, with my waterproofs still damp and my squelching footsteps muffled by the patter of rain against my jacket's hood, I set

To be at the mercy of the changing seasons like this and to notice the subtle day-to-day shifts in a landscape makes you aware of your own rhythms, your own desire to seek comfort and warmth

off along a small portion of the 77-mile-long Rob Roy Way, which follows the route the outlaw once trod. A few hours from my whisky-serving end-point, The Falls of Dochart Inn, I looked over the misty valley from the Glen Ogle Viaduct (part of a disused railway line) and accepted that there's an art to embracing a landscape in bad weather. You're not seeing it at its postcard-perfect-best, but you are witnessing the seasons at work.

As the elements might suggest, I was journeying through the National Park in autumn, a time when the oak trees glow yellow and Munros that weeks earlier had been blanketed in purple heather are now rust and umber. To be at the mercy of the changing seasons like this and to notice the subtle day-to-day shifts in a landscape makes you aware of your own rhythms, your own desire to seek

comfort and warmth. It was far removed from the madcap exhilaration of high summer when you can spend hours chasing sunsets, your body fuelled by the abundance of light.

I spent my last Trossachs day at Bracklinn Falls, a short drive (or uphill walk) from the market town of Callander. Here, I realised that rain has other benefits, with the waterfall transformed into something fierce and spectacular after the deluge. Standing by it, I witnessed nature's forces at work, appreciating how these rocks have been carved out over aeons by the course of dark, tumultuous water. Wild weather may slow you down by ruling out more extensive routes and dubious scrambles, but it can also make everything else seem more vivid and alive.

(right) One of Loch Lomond and the Trossachs National Park's numerous waterfalls, which look particularly wild and wonderful after a bout of rain

DIRECTORY

While Loch Lomond and the Trossachs are fabulous in wet weather,
don't be afraid to visit when the sun shines. Repeat trips are easy,
given that the National Park is only a short drive from Glasgow.

STAY

Kip Hideaways: The Treehouses at Lanrick

Slumber 20 feet above native Scottish wood-land in one of these five larch-clad treehouses, all of which come complete with impossibly soft beds, outdoor copper bathtubs, quirky details (like walls made from salvaged windows and doors) and sweeping verandas. The site itself stands beside the Teith River (ideal for otter and red-squirrel spotting, or a custom fishing experience) and features a birch-framed sauna and plunge pool. Two of the treehouses are linked by a rope-bridge, making them fun and family-friendly, and you can arrange to have your fridges filled with goodies from the Blair Drummond Smiddy Farm Shop.

kiphideaways.com/hideaways/trossachs-treehouses
Lanrick, Nr Doune, Perthshire FK16 6HJ

Kip Hideaways: Caban Dubh

This bolthole, found at the northeast edge of the National Park, offers secluded calm. Start the day with a dunk in the cold water therapy barrel or simply lounge in bed looking out across the farm and hills. Nearby Loch Earn is great for paddleboarding, while Ben Vorlich calls to those keen to bag a Munro.

kiphideaways.com/hideaways/loch-earn-cabin-scotland
Caban Dubh, Westview, St Fillans, Perthshire PH6 2NQ

Cameron House

A ten-minute drive from the chocolate-box village of Luss, on the shores of Loch Lomond, this lush, 208-room hotel is perfect for those travelling with little ones in tow. With a slide-adorned pool, on-site cinema, sprawling grounds, outdoor activities and family suites decked out with board games, there's buckets of built-in entertainment. The hotel restaurants all offer kids' menus, including Cameron Grill, with its classic Scottish offerings, and The Boat House, renowned for its seafood.

cameronhouse.co.uk
Loch Lomond, Alexandria G83 8QZ

EAT

Mhor Bread & Store

A bakery has stood on this spot along the Callander Main Street for more than a cen-tury, and Mhor Bread keeps baking traditions alive by only using Scottish-milled flour in their sourdough, which you can buy alongside hearty sandwiches, moreish cakes, soups and award-winning pies.

mhorbread.net
8 Main St, Callander FK17 8BB

Falls of Dochart Inn

Named after the waterfall it sits beside, this revamped historic coaching inn boasts an on-site smokehouse, whitewashed dining room and a traditional bar filled with candles and the odd Jacobean sword.

fallsofdochart.co.uk
Gray St, Killin FK21 8SL

The Drovers Inn

Perched at the narrower northern end of Loch Lomond, this is a great spot for hikers in need of a dram (and a view). Opened in 1705, it counts Samuel Johnson as a past guest and is said to be haunted by a 300-year-old ghost called Angus, an ill-fated drover.

droversinn.co.uk
North Loch Lomond, Inverarnan G83 7DX

The Glenturret Lalique Restaurant

If you're driving to the National Park from Edinburgh, break up the journey at The Glenturret, Scotland's oldest working distillery and home to the Glenturret Lalique Restaurant, which has two Michelin stars. With only seven tables, the classic interiors are a dashing stage for the Lalique lights, glasses, decanters and vases – and the fabulous meal. If you can't stay for dinner, book a bar lunch, featuring dishes like cauliflower dusted with truffle and Shetland cod balanced by black pudding, alongside a collection of 400 whiskies.

theglenturretrestaurant.com
Glenturret Distillery, The, Hosh, Crieff PH7 4HA

DO

Long Distance Walks

Loch Lomond and the Trossachs National Park is crisscrossed with trails, some delivering you to the top of Munros, others taking you to tumbling waterfalls hidden among woodland. Then there are long-distance legends like the Rob Roy Way and John Muir Way, the latter named for the Father of National Parks, a nat-uralist who appreciated the power of wildness and soaring peaks. The most popular route (explored by around 100,000 walkers every year) is the 95-mile-long West Highland Way, which stretches from Milngavie (just north of Glasgow) to Fort William. The walk winds along an old drover's trail on Loch Lomond's eastern shore, and although the full trail requires around a week to conquer, the time-strapped can join for a shorter ramble – the stretch from Balmaha up along the loch is particularly lovely.

Kip Hideaways: The Treehouses at Lanrick

The Glenturret Distillery

The Glenturret Lalique Restaurant

Kip Hideaways: Caban Dubh

Falls of Dochart Inn

Cameron House, Lobby Bar and Library

OBAN
AND MULL

Time with a landscape and community shaped by the sea

Photographs by Chiara Dalla Rosa

Oban owes everything to the sea, with the waves bringing language, trade and the country's Gaelic heritage. It was here that the Scoti first arrived from Northern Ireland, going on to found the ancient Kingdom of Dalriada (now Argyle), with clan leaders assuming the imposing title of Lords of the Isles. Visiting today, it's clear that Oban remains entwined with the sea. The surrounding coastline is scattered with secluded bays and caves backed by forests and cliffs. And in Oban itself, set beside Loch Laich, the waterfront is the town's beating heart, lined with seafood restaurants, galleries, granite houses and a

distillery where whisky is flavoured by the salt air. But to really understand how the sea can shape a community, you need to spend time on an island. Conveniently, Oban is one of Scotland's biggest tourist ports, with CalMac Ferries venturing to the nearby isles of Coll, Tiree, Lismore, Kerrera and Colonsay – and to my chosen destination, Mull, an hour-long sail away.

Slow travel is all about finding ways to connect, with a landscape, a community and the culture and traditions that allow a place to thrive. Keen to understand the nuances of island living, I decided to spend my time getting to know one small corner

of the island: Mull's southern tip. I drove past the clifftop Duart Castle (ancestral home of the Macleans since the 13th century) and the turn off to Carsaig Arches (eroded basalt formations that resemble portals to other realms), and eventually arrived in the small port town of Fionnphort.

The first people I met were my hosts, Hannah Fisher and Sorren Maclean, musicians who'd transformed a run-down shed into the two-person, impeccably designed Fairwinds Cabin, part of the Kip Hideaways collection. As we drank tea in the cabin's garden (where I was frequently distracted by waterfalls that appeared to flow upwards, buffeted by the wind across the bay), Sorren laughed about how the elements really do dictate everything here. 'Whether it's a beautiful day or a horrendous day, you're still very connected to the sea,' he says. 'You have to plan your week around the weather, and it makes you appreciate the seasons. There's a rule that if it's sunny, you have to go and enjoy it because that might be it for the rest of the year.'

'I love everything about life in Mull,' adds Hannah, pointing out that islanders prefer the term 'in Mull' over 'on Mull', which comes from the Gaelic where you live *in* a place rather than simply on it. 'We have a little boat and that's one of my favourite things: just heading out on a calm evening and sitting with a glass of wine, watching the sun set with no one else around. But I also love that there's a different kind of community on the island. Everyone makes an effort to do their bit, to be there for each other, to check in.'

On an island, community is vital. You need to know and be there for those around you – a necessity when living somewhere remote. And this sense of togetherness gives rise to a powerful collective identity. 'There's a connection you feel when you meet other islanders,' Hannah explains. 'Perhaps it's a Hebridean thing, because we can survive the winters, but there is a craic that only islanders have. It's like a whole other language.'

Hannah and Sorren are singers (they met gigging in Glasgow), yet like everyone in Mull, they wear many hats. Artists might be in the coastguard, farmers could man the ferry, and those working the looms at the Ardalanish weaving mill may be behind the bar at The Keel Row, where Hannah and Sorren often play sessions. Moreover, as ferry crossings can be tricky and storms can cut them off entirely, islanders also need to know how to fix things – and if you can't fix something, you most likely know someone who can. Repair someone's chainsaw and they'll sort out your gate; catch a lobster (as Sorren did recently) and swap it for a pair of Wellies.

I'm not quite as self-sufficient as the locals, so I needed someone to catch my seafood supper. This is how I met Neil MacLeod Jardine, who helms Iona Seafood and sells his catch directly from his boat, which lands at Fionnphort pier and over in Iona, his home – an island so close to Fionnphort that I could see its abbey when I met Neil to pick up my crab and langoustines.

'I've always enjoyed being on the water, so fishing was just an extension of that,' Neil says, as he wrangles with a lobster. 'I think about lots of things on the boat, about fishing-related stuff, but also about family, what I'm seeing, what's happening later in the year. You're always working out there, but you have time to think.'

The exceptional seafood is one of the things that drew me to this part of Scotland. Its brilliance comes down to the clean water, which is fed by the Gulf Stream – this makes the water warmer than similar latitudes on the east coast and helps things grow quickly. But it's more than the water's riches that tie Neil to the island; it's the safety of Iona, the fact that his daughter can play on the same beaches he did as a child, and the sense of community. 'Iona gets very busy in the summer, so you've got this constant flow of people,' he explains. 'There's staff who come and work in the hotels, some come back year after year, and some have never been before. That keeps the social side of things interesting. It keeps it vibrant.'

Dutch artist, writer and bookmaker Miek Zwamborn and her partner Rutger Emmelkamp, a teacher and artist, were two such arrivals. They came to Mull for a holiday, then unexpectedly

(right) Iona; The Lismore Island ferry at Port Appin, near Oban

It's more than the water's riches that keeps Neil on the island; it's the safety of Iona, the fact that his daughter can play on the same beaches he did as a child, and the sense of community

agreed to stay for a year and look after the house of a local they met fishing. Nearly a decade later, they are slowly rewilding their island patch and have founded KNOCKvologan, a space where they host creative residencies for nature-focused artists, writers and researchers. All stays culminate in a public event, be it an exhibition, workshop, concert or open studio.

'The idea behind the residencies was to have conversations with the community here and bring in experts from around the world,' says Rutger. 'It's so great to make work that's connected to a place physically, and to emphasise art's social aspect: how it can hopefully help make change by encouraging people to look at the landscape in different ways.'

For Miek and Rutger, the rhythms and rituals of Mull have changed their understanding of what it means to be connected. 'We help our neighbour with his sheep, even though we're edging towards a plant-based diet. Our personal convictions don't always matter because people are more important, your neighbours are more important. There's so much of that here.'

As I get older, I've started to realise that the travel memories that stick all involve a moment of connection – something as simple as an ephemeral conversation with a stranger about how it feels to be awed by a landscape, or a seascape for that matter. In Oban and Mull, it's all about connection – to the past, the land, your community – and perhaps that's why life by the sea, despite all the hardships and history, has always seemed so appealing to me. And why I can't wait to go back.

(left) Fisherman Neil MacLeod Jardine, Fionnphort

DIRECTORY

Many of Mull's businesses operate seasonally and close during the winter months. If you're planning to visit off-season, make sure to check what is open in advance.

STAY

Kip Hideaways: Fairwinds Cabin

This grass-roofed cabin is filled with charming details, from Ross Ryan's almost abstract canvases (which he paints from the deck of his fishing boat) to floorboards salvaged from a Glasgow church and an old high school desk repurposed as a kitchen countertop. The bed is even inspired by a traditional Hebridean box bed, once shared by an entire family (although here you have it all to yourself). Make sure to throw open the curtains every now and then to check if the Northern Lights are putting on a show.

kiphideaways.com/hideaways/mull-cabin
Fairwinds Cabin, Knockan, Isle of Mull PA67 6DN

Inverlonan Bothies

Cocooned among ancient oaks, Inverlonan's collection of striking bothies have been created in partnership with local craftspeople. They offer a taste of off-grid living (requiring a buggy, walk or boat across Loch Nell to reach), but come with a host of welcome comforts, including a sauna, breakfast hampers, wood-fired pizza oven and outdoor shower.

inverlonan.com
Inverlonan, Ballygowan Farm, Oban PA34 4QE

EAT

The Seafood Hut

The bright-green Seafood Hut was founded by Marion Ritchie and John Ogden, a pioneering prawn skipper who was the first to proclaim Oban Scotland's seafood capital. Working with local fishers who catch lobster, crab, scallops and mussels to order, the fare is fresh and affordable. Waiting in line, you'll likely be given a mussel or two to snack on, cooked outdoors in white wine and garlic, and their seafood platter pairs perfectly with a glass of delicate and citrusy Oban 14 whisky, which you can pick up on a distillery tour further along the waterfront.

Calmac Pier, Oban PA34 4DB

The Pierhouse

Outside, a blue ferry pootles back and forth across Loch Linnhe to Lismore Island. Inside, the fire crackles, whisky bottles line the bar and David Shrigley prints share the wall with vintage travel posters urging you to see Scotland by train. Head Chef Michael Leathley champions local suppliers, including Eoghan Black and his Loch Linnhe langoustines, and Judith Vajk from the family-run Caledonian Oyster Co in nearby Loch Creran.

pierhousehotel.co.uk/eat-with-us
The Pier House, Port Appin, Appin PA38 4DE

Iona Seafood, Fionnphort & Iona

Neil MacLeod catches, packages and sells his sustainable catch directly from his boat at the Fionnphort and Iona piers. His fruits de mer are as fresh as they come, and for those daunted by the prospect of de-shelling prawns, he suggests embracing the messy fun of it all and mucking in over a bottle of wine.

www.ionaseafood.com

Ninth Wave Restaurant

Carla Lamont came to Iona 30 years ago expecting to stay for a season. But then she met Johnny, 'the sexy Scottish fisherman', who cooked her a lobster dinner and made leaving impossible. The couple now run Ninth Wave, a bothy-turned-restaurant surrounded by Mull moorland where Carla creates dishes using Johnny's catch and ingredients grown in their crofting garden. In keeping with the island ethos, they want guests to feel as if they're at a dinner party where they just don't know the hosts yet, and Carla's flavour combinations are inspired by the couple's extensive travels.

ninthwaverestaurant.co.uk
Bruach Mhor Fionnphort, Mull PA66 6BL

DO

The Islands

To sample some of the smaller islands off Oban and Mull, catch a ferry to Lunga (one of the Treshnish Isles) for the puffins, or to the once-volcanic Staffa, which is found on the same fault as Northern Ireland's Giant's Causeway and is renowned for its towering basalt formations, like the cathedralesque, 226-foot-deep Fingal's Cave.

Iona, a short sail from Fionnphort, is home to the abbey founded by the exiled Irish monk St Columba (of *Book of Kells* fame) in 563. Rebuilt over the centuries, the Iona Abbey remains a pilgrimage site, although travellers today are also likely to be walkers (hike up Dun I for the view) and geology enthusiasts, who come for the Iona greenstone and 2,000-million-year-old Lewisian Gneiss (too old, even, to contain fossils).

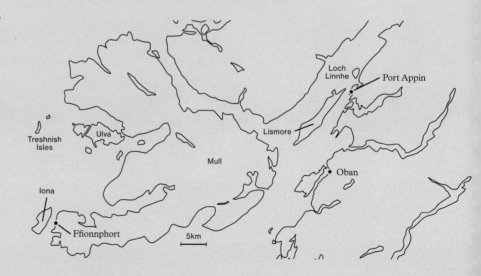

The Seafood Hut

Ninth Wave Restaurant

The Pierhouse

Whisky samples from Oban Distillery

View from the Kip Hideaways: Fairwinds Cabin

Inverlonan Bothies

Iona Abbey

ISLE OF SKYE

A majestic island with a dark history

Photographs by Holly Farrier

It doesn't take much for your imagination to run wild on Skye, an island in the Inner Hebrides with 7,000 miles of coast and around 500 million years of history. Scattered with dinosaur footprints and ruined Pictish brochs (Iron Age stone structures), this was once the domain of Vikings and warriors, including one who gave his heart to a fairy. And although Skye (the second largest of Scotland's 790-odd islands) remains jaw-droppingly stunning, there's a poetic darkness here, too.

It was to Skye that Bonnie Prince Charlie (Charles Edward Stuart) fled after the catastrophic Battle of Culloden in 1746 failed to return the British crown to the House of Stuart. Following this military blow, Skye's inhabitants were cruelly subjugated by the British Government. The clan system ended, tartan and Gaelic were outlawed and many crofters (seen as a hindrance to the growing sheep industry) were forcibly evicted during the Highland Clearances of the 18th and 19th centuries. But through all this, nature remained a sublime constant. Today, when rolling sea mists break, the true majesty of the island's mountainous backbone, dominated by the Black Cuillin, is revealed. There are glimpses of

To really experience Skye's windswept isolation, you should travel by foot

volcanic stacks and craggy pinnacles, the afternoon light softening these harsh formations until they resemble crumpled blankets, perhaps left by long-forgotten giants.

Caught up in the natural splendour, it can take time to see how history has shaped this landscape. But venture out with an islander and soon enough rows of tumbledown rocks revert to Viking fortifications and grassy mounds transform into cottages swallowed by the earth. Outdoor guide Mitchell Partridge helped me decode Skye's terrain. Based in Carbost, not far from the Talisker distillery, Mitchell is the man (and forager) behind guiding company Skye Ghillie, leading expeditions, hikes and fishing trips along the brilliantly named River Snizort and beyond. Acting as a gatekeeper to a forgotten Skye, he offers guests the chance to encounter eagles and otters, while gaining a deeper understanding of this ancient, changeable island and those who made it their home. 'I can stand among the ruins and feel the presence of the people there,' Mitchell says. 'I like showing people the old walls and black houses and saying: this desolate land, you may think it's beautiful and that no one lives here, but they did. Once every glen had a settlement. I still feel a connection to those who were here just by the tangible evidence that we have in the land – the scars and old walls.

'I love telling people about the island and seeing the surprise on their faces when I tell them about the population in 1841, and how much smaller it is now. I love the world coming here and going away

(overleaf) Camasunary Bay

with a little more knowledge. You get a smell, a feel and literally a taste of what the island has to offer. That's something you can't pick up in a book; it's tangible, it's boots on the ground.'

With roads and laneways leading to white-sand beaches and Jurassic mountains, driving is a great way to see all this island has to offer – but to really experience Skye's windswept isolation, you should also stop, as often as you can, and travel by foot. Portree, on the Trotternish Peninsula, with its harbour flanked by cray pots and flamboyantly coloured houses, is the island's cultural hub, and a great place to start an expedition. Driving north, the A855 takes you past rolling pastures and ubiquitous Highland cattle to Uig, where ferries set off for the isles of Uist and Harris. Here, you can walk to Rha Burn, a double waterfall, and Eyre's standing stones. Or there's the Fairy Glen, a mass of grassy hills and ponds (topped by Castle Ewan, a ruin-like natural rock formation) that could easily be mistaken for a mythical realm.

For a taste of Jacobite history, drive on to Kilmuir, where Flora MacDonald's headstone stands tall, its epitaph lauding this revered figure who aided Bonnie Prince Charlie in his escape to Skye. Nearby is his hiding place, Duntulm Castle, now a solitary ruin. At this point, the coast-hugging road turns south, past cliffs and stone-lined craters that were once village sheep pens, to Staffin, then gets narrower and narrower as it twists around folded hills to the soaring Quiraing. This still-moving landslip has created a magnificent collection of crags and bluffs that beg to be scrambled over.

History is everywhere on Skye and, once you learn how to read the landscape, conjuring it becomes easy

Further west, on the Waternish Peninsula, is Dunvegan Castle, home to the MacLeods for more than 800 years (which makes it Scotland's oldest continually inhabited castle). On display among the family's furniture, art and antiques is the Fairy Flag (*Am Bratach Sith*), thought by some to be a gift from a fairy bride to her chieftain husband when she was forced to return to fairyland. Believed to guarantee victory if waved in battle thanks to its magical powers, MacLeod pilots carried photos of it during the First World War. It's far more likely, though, that the flag was once the banner of the Norwegian King Harald Hardrada, who came (and failed) to conquer England and has ancestral links to the Chiefs of MacLeod.

From the castle, it's a short journey to Claigan where you can amble through meadows and around crumbling stone walls (evidence, as always, of Skye's past) to a whitish-pink coral beach that's surprisingly tropical when the sun shines. On the other side of Loch Dunvegan is Neist Point, where the steep walk to its stoic lighthouse – the most westerly on Skye – is a blustery but invigorating affair. If you're after something more strenuous (and higher vantage points) then brave the Cuillin mountain range – something best done with a guide. Of course, there's always the iconic Old Man of Storr walk, which is both busy and beautiful.

History is everywhere on Skye and, once you learn how to read the landscape, conjuring it becomes easy. When travelling back to Inverness (the ideal starting point for any Highland odyssey) via the Applecross Peninsula you pass over Scotland's highest road, the single lane, hairpin-bend-filled Bealach na Bà. Your heart may be in your mouth, but the view across to the Outer Hebrides is enough to inspire the ascent. Here, the land once again bears signs of human enterprise. There are dips and rises in place of crofts, you imagine that folds in the terrain could have once hidden distilleries and even the road's name is a nod to its droving past, translating as 'the pass of the cattle'. Reading the landscape like this, pondering the tales behind stone walls and uneven ground, makes the present infinitely more fascinating.

DIRECTORY

There is no airport on Skye, so it's best to start your journey from Inverness, which will allow you to drive through the Applecross Peninsula on your way to the island (a slightly indirect route, but worth the detour). You can also catch the ferry from Maillaig.

STAY

Kinloch Lodge

This award-winning boutique hotel and restaurant holds court on the shores of Loch Na Dal. Home to the Macdonald family for five generations, it is filled with roaring fires, cosy rooms and ancestral memorabilia. Lady Claire and Lord Godfrey Macdonald (the hotel is now helmed by their daughter Isabella) opened Kinloch Lodge in 1972, when the journey from Edinburgh to Skye often took 12 hours. While things might be more accessible today, you'll still feel as if you've come to the end of the world – and the sense of seclusion (mixed with Highland hospitality) is truly restorative. Claire put Kinloch on the foodie map five decades ago and the team still showcase the bounty found on their doorstep, with the dinner menu changing nightly.

kinloch-lodge.co.uk
A851, Sleat, Isle of Skye IV43 8QY

Harlosh Wood h

Blending into the surrounding fields and boasting phenomenal coastal views, this architecturally designed, self-catering six-person bolthole is inspired by a traditional Scottish longhouse. Furnishings are sleek and snug, floors are oak, contemporary artworks mirror the Skye seascape and stargazing from the sweeping terrace is astounding. Far away from the glow of any city, it's so crisp and clear here that you can make out the clouds of the Milky Way. For something more intimate, there's also the minimalist, croft-framed Black h, a sister property that sleeps just two and has equally remarkable views.

harlosh.co/wood-h
Lower Milovaig, Glendale, Isle of Skye IV55 8WR

Eagle Brae

If you start your journey in Inverness, spend a few nights getting used to nature's rhythms at Eagle Brae, a collection of grass-roofed wood cabins on the 8,000-acre Struy Estate, a 40-minute drive from the city. Owners Mike and Pawana Spencer-Nairn wanted to create a Scottish-Himalayan mountain village on the land which has been in Mike's family since the 1930s. Their cabins (no two are identical) feature an original assortment of ornate carvings depicting animals, Scottish motifs and Celtic gods, created by Pawana's brother-in-law, a master woodcutter. Enclosed by Highland glens, protected wildflower grasslands and the salmon-filled River Glass, wildlife comes right to your door. British raptors, golden eagles and red kites fly overhead, and Right to Roam means you can wander almost anywhere on the Estate.

eaglebrae.co.uk
Eagle Brae, Struy IV4 7LE

EAT

The Three Chimneys

Set within a revamped, lochside crofter's cottage, this restaurant is the jewel in Skye's fine dining crown. Ingredients are sourced from the island's 'natural larder', and since much of the surrounding land and sea is a designated wilderness area, the award-winning food is garden (and ocean) fresh.

threechimneys.co.uk
Colbost, Dunvegan, Colbost, Isle of Skye IV55 8ZT

Chidakasha

Brave a serpentine single-lane road to reach this relaxed vegetarian restaurant. Beloved by locals, meals feature organic vegetables alongside flowers and herbs harvested from the on-site croft, and dishes are paired with tea from around the world.

chidakashaskye.co.uk
Holmisdale, Glendale, Isle of Skye IV55 8WS

Scorrybreac

Chef Calum Munro named his restaurant Scorrybreac (Gaelic for 'speckled rock') after his parent's stone cottage – which is fitting, given that he first opened it in their front room. Now found in a stone terrace above the harbour, Calum's inventive menu is shaped by his time working in France and makes use of everything from Skye venison to foraged sea vegetables.

scorrybreac.com
7 Bosville Terrace, Portree IV51 9DG

Birch

Known for its brilliant cakes and perfectly brewed coffee, this Scandi-esque cafe looks out onto Donnie Munro's striking murals depicting Skye landmarks like Neist Point and the Old Man of Storr.

birch-skye.co
Bayfield Rd, Portree IV51 9EL

DO

The Sleat Peninsula

The landscape at the southern end of Skye is a mix of forested glens, sprawling moors and crofting townships enjoying splendid isolation. Follow the steep, winding road past the surprisingly warm, swimmer-friendly Torrin Pools to Elgol, a tiny fishing village with views back to the Black Cuillin. Elgol's pier is the starting point for wildlife cruises to puffin-occupied destinations like Canna and Loch Coruisk, although relatively fine weather is required to venture out. Torabhaig, Skye's newest distillery, is also found on Sleat, as is the walker-beloved Point of Sleat and Dunscaith Castle.

sleatperfectlyskye.com

Òr

Found in the heart of Portree, every piece in this design store has a story, with owner (and jewellery designer) Jennifer Pearson keen to promote emerging artisans and those inspired by the island.

orskye.com
4 Wentworth St, Portree IV51 9EJ

Skye Ghillie

Guide (and history-buff) Mitchell Partridge leads small tours across Skye, focusing on the island's past, wildlife and natural riches. This is a great day out for fans of fishing and foraging.

skyeghillie.com

Eagle Brae

The Sleat Peninsula

Kinloch Lodge Dining Room

Dunscaith Castle

Dunvegan Castle

Kinloch Lodge

Birch

On the Eagle Brae grounds

Harlosh Wood h

ISLAY

Drink whisky with the Queen of the Hebrides

Photographs by Chiara Dalla Rosa

Whisper the word 'Islay' to a whisky lover and you'll set their heart aflutter, for this is where you venture when keen to understand the nuances of terroir (the way the climate, soil, terrain and tradition shape flavour) while imbibing a few drams somewhere sublime.

Located off Scotland's west coast, the island of Islay wears the title of 'Queen of the Hebrides' well. Home to around 3,000 people, it is a place of grandeur and tradition, where fishing communities thrive, Gaelic is still spoken and the land is incredibly fertile, making it ideal for growing barley. Add peat bogs, moorland and pristine

water, and you have all the ingredients required for whisky. It's little wonder, then, that Islay, where the whisky-producing style is protected by law, is home to nine distilleries – plus another on Jura, a narrow, lesser-tramped island a five-minute sail away.

Travelling between the distilleries takes you on a grand tour of Islay's stunning attractions, from the azure waters of Port Ellen and the havens of Machir and Saligo Bay, to the Mull of Oa, reached via a path which begins at the American Monument, erected to commemorate two US battleships that sunk nearby in the First

This is a place of grandeur and tradition,
where fishing communities thrive, Gaelic is
still spoken and the land is incredibly fertile

World War. And while distillery-hopping is the best way to experience the island, it also gives you a chance to look behind the scenes and learn that no two whiskies are alike – and that production here is a labour of love.

My desire to explore Islay was sparked by a conversation with Katy Fennema, whisky ambassador at The Fife Arms Hotel in the Cairngorms National Park, on the other side of the country. A regular Islay visitor, Katy believes that the island's power lies in its peat. 'In different parts of Scotland, peat is composed of different things,' she says. 'Peat from the Cairngorms has sphagnum moss in it, whereas on Orkney it has a lot of heather, so you get these floral, honey notes. On Islay, their peat has had the waves of the Atlantic lashing against it for the last 10,000 years, so it's salty. And on really stormy days there will be a bit of seaweed splashed onto it too, so we get those medicinal iodine notes. It's a totally different whisky.

'Islay is an incredibly welcoming island that has, to a big extent, been built around its distilleries, which contribute so much to the community,' Katy continues. 'You turn a corner and there's another distillery, and another. You've got Ardbeg, Lagavulin and Laphroaig on the south coast; and I love Bruichladdich [on Islay's west coast], which has been given the freedom to explore terroir.'

I understood Katy's ardour. Years before, I'd spoken to Bruichladdich's then-Master Distiller, Jim McEwan, and immediately fell for the ethos as much as the taste. Jim is an Islay native who

began working in 1963, aged 15, as a trainee cooper (barrel maker) at the island's Bowmore Distillery. Now retired, he played a vital role in resurrecting Bruichladdich distillery in 2001, after it had been abandoned for years, and in crafting the signature flavour – although much of this is dictated by Islay itself.

'All our Bruichladdich casks are matured on the island,' Jim explained to me at the time. 'The air is different. We are surrounded by the Atlantic Ocean and the winds coming in are laden with salt. The barley growing on the island puts its roots down deep into the Islay soil, which is loaded with salt. The rain that falls on the barley is salty rain. The casks are breathing this all the time, and it gives our spirit a citrus, marine freshness. And the hand of man is there as well. The guys have come up from generation after generation of distillers and farmers: an unbroken chain of people who have been born and raised on this island of whisky. It's in their DNA and they respect it; they know the value of making good whisky. [Islay is] a distilling island. This is what we do best.'

Much of Islay's unique flavour is introduced via the essential ingredients. The barley used by many distilleries often grows in peat bog (a byproduct of the west coast's famously damp weather), which also infuses the water in springs and streams. And the distinctive Islay smokiness can also be enhanced by using peat during malting.

(previous) Peat at Laphroaig; Preparing for a tasting at Laphroaig
(right) The Islay coastline

*To taste something made with so much love and care,
while talking to those who have dedicated their lives
to distilling, helps you understand whisky's allure*

This is an early step in the whisky-making operation where barley is soaked in cold water, then drained and left to germinate – a process that is stopped, at just the right point, by hot air, created in some cases by burning peat.

What might surprise you most, tasting and smelling your way around the island, is that while whisky is made from the same core elements (grain, water, yeast), all sourced from a small patch of land, each distillery still has its own flavour. Despite being the most peated of all Islay's malts, Ardbeg whisky is sweet and floral, the creamy texture created by wooden washbacks (fermentation containers) rather than the more common steel. Laphroaig varieties come with a hint of seaweed that makes it almost medicinal, and in salty Lagavulin you can taste plants like bog myrtle and a sherry sweetness, a flavour added by the casks the spirit is aged in.

To taste something made with so much love and care, while talking to those who have dedicated their lives to distilling, helps you understand whisky's allure – and just how beloved this island and industry are. 'Islay is ruggedly beautiful,' says Jackie Thomson, Distillery Visitor Centre Manager at Ardbeg. 'I love the wildness of the island and the way your mood changes with the weather. There is an unpredictability to Islay... nature throws its best and worst at you, sometimes in one day. You can stand on a beach and not see a soul in the biting wind, then you can visit a distillery and be in the throng of visitors from all over the world. You can hear the roar of stags, bob around on a boat, be in the midst of a whisky festival, walk in silence for hours, wild swim or dance until you cannot stop at a ceilidh.'

Jim McEwan shared this zeal for his remote and resilient home. 'I've been around the world more times than Phileas Fogg but there's something about this island,' he told me. 'The thing I miss most when I'm travelling is the sound of the sea. It's a constant in our lives here. We have beautiful silences, tranquility, wildness and storms. I was on the west coast in a gale force nine and all I wanted to do was watch the waves come in. I'm sitting there freezing, but I've got a flask of coffee and some shortbread and I'm looking at the waves that have come all the way from Canada. The power of nature – people should witness this.'

It may be the whisky talking, but I appreciate how Islay can get under your skin. You come to witness the alchemy at work in far-flung distilleries but leave with more – an awareness of how landscapes can shape flavour, tradition and community, and a desire to spend more time with the waves.

DIRECTORY

Islay can be reached by sailing with Calmac Ferries from Oban and Kennacraig (and then on to Jura), or by flying from Glasgow.

STAY

The Machrie Hotel
Islay has more than 130 miles of coastline, so embrace the setting and stay beside the Atlantic in this 47-room hotel. Its sleek interiors are brightened by contemporary art and immense windows that make the most of the surroundings, a soothing mix of water and farmland. From here, set off on a guided sea kayak tour or spend a morning on The Machrie's iconic golf course, which has stood beside the dunes since 1891.

themachrie.com
Port Ellen, Isle of Islay PA42 7AN

Camping
There are a few established campsites on Islay, but as this is Scotland, wild camping might also appeal – after all, few things are better than sleeping beneath the stars or waking to the sound of rain on canvas. Right to Roam gives the adventurous freedom to walk and camp where they please, but take care to only stay for a few nights in one place, steer clear of animals and agricultural land, eschew open fires (especially on peaty soil) and leave no trace.

EAT

Old Kiln Cafe, Ardbeg
Not all distillery eateries are created equal, and Ardbeg is one that gets things right. Dine year-round at the peat-scented Old Kiln Cafe, which is found where the distillery's old malting floors once stood (the whisky cheesecake is delectable). You can also pick up staples like soups and sandwiches from the alfresco ARDstream Trailer in summer.

ardbeg.com
Isle of Islay PA42 7EA

Peatzeria
Worth frequenting for the pun alone, Peatzeria is found within a revamped Episcopalian church (vaulted ceilings and all) overlooking Loch Indaal. While this pizza restaurant dishes up a range of Italian classics, it's worth ordering something loaded with Islay seafood and eating your fare by the water's edge.

peatzeria.com
22 Shore St, Bowmore, Isle of Islay PA43 7LB

The Bars
The snug, award-winning Islay Whisky Bar at the Ballygrant Inn has a whisky list made up of more than 900 tipples, so settling in for the evening is remarkably tempting. Drams can also be savoured at the Port Charlotte Hotel's wood-carved bar, which hosts regular trad music nights and has views across to the Paps of Jura.

ballygrant-inn.com | Ballygrant, Isle of Islay PA45 7QR
portcharlottehotel.co.uk | Main St, Port Charlotte,
  Isle of Islay PA48 7TU

DO

The Distilleries:
Most of Islay's distilleries offer tours and tastings (it's always best to book ahead), and I have a fondness for Ardbeg, Lagavulin, Laphroaig and Bruichladdich. The first three of these are connection by the Three Distilleries Path, which is great to walk or cycle.

Glasgow
If you're travelling to Islay via Glasgow, take your time in the city and pay your respects to the father of Scottish Arts & Crafts, Charles Rennie Mackintosh. A designer, architect and artist, Charles (together with his brilliant wife Margaret Macdonald, a fellow pioneer of the Glasgow Style) created singular Art Nouveau homes and interiors that doubled as functional artworks. Mackintosh pilgrims keen to see the couple's inventive, nature-inspired work should visit The Hill House, The Willow Tea Rooms, Mackintosh Queen's Cross Church, The Lighthouse and House For An Art Lover.

Old Kiln Cafe, Ardbeg

The Machrie Hotel

Laphroaig Distillery

Ardbeg Distillery

The Machrie Hotel

NORTH COAST 500

A meandering road trip through rugged landscape

Photographs by Chiara Dalla Rosa

I could see Ullapool's Rhue Lighthouse from the start of the walk, which looked like an easy stroll through waist-high ferns that were slowly turning from emerald to rust. But as the clouds rumbled over Loch Broom and the bemused sheep huddled ever closer on the rocky beach below me, the heavens opened. All I could hear above the rush of wind were my sodden boots squelching through the mud; I'd given up any hope of my feet remaining dry days ago. Yet ten minutes later, standing soaked but elated on a sandstone outcrop at the lighthouse's base, tranquillity returned. The sun shone, the foliage

glowed and I convinced myself that I could make out the distant shape of the Summer Isles just off to the north. On Scotland's west coast the weather changes fast, but the North Coast 500 (also known as the NC500) is fabulous in every element.

Starting in Inverness, this 516-mile circular driving route (inevitable detours make it longer) takes in a plethora of Highland icons, from lively hubs like Ullapool to cliffside castle ruins glaring out towards Orkney. But what makes the NC500 astounding is that so much can be seen along the road itself, from forests, Munros and mossy trails

to hillsides streaked with waterfalls. You don't need playlists to pass the hours – the landscape does it for you.

There are countless ways to make the NC500 your own, but if you want to follow my journey, start by driving northeast from Inverness. Spend your morning wandering the ruins of Urquhart Castle on the shores of Loch Ness, drive on to the thundering, whisky-hued Rogie Falls and then end the day by rolling into the port town of Ullapool, ready for a chilled al fresco feast at The Seafood Shack.

The area north of Ullapool is a geologist's dream, the road taking you through valleys ripped open by glaciers and terrain carved out by deserts and ancient oceans. This is one of the oldest landscapes in Europe, where peaks are marked by folds and fault lines, and it's fascinating to see something so ancient paired with signs of human life. Whitewashed cottages sit like beacons at the base of Munros, while Ardvreck (a skeletal island castle dating from the 15th century) seems to be sinking into the loch.

To get to grips with the earth (geology has always boggled me), I paid a visit to Highland Stoneware, a Lochinver ceramics studio and shop founded in 1974. Part of their collection is crafted using geo-glazes, made with crushed rocks from the region. These include 3,000-million-year-old Lewisian Gneiss, which began life as magma, and Ullapool limestone, which is around 500 million years old and took shape in warm, shallow seas. The latter melts during firing and then crystallises as it cools, creating an almost opal-like effect.

Having watched the ceramicists at work (you can walk through the space, striking up conversations as artisans sculpt and paint), I hit the road again, keen to get back into the landscape that inspired these pieces. Lochinver lies within the UNESCO-listed North West Highlands Geopark, which covers 772 square miles, is scattered with that ancient Lewisian Gneiss and is filled with a range of self-guided walks. Continuing all the way to Cape Wrath in the far northwest (the starting point for the decidedly unforgiving 200-mile-long Cape Wrath Trail), the Geopark also contains

the Moine Thrust Zone, an immense geological structure which helped prove that the continents collided. Then there's the considerably more modern hermit's castle. This tiny, almost Brutalist structure (said to be the smallest castle in Europe) is built on the exposed, sheep-dotted headland above the crescent-shaped Achmelvich Beach – a calm, crystalline haven come summer.

The next NC500 stretch delivered me to Wailing Widow Falls, less than an hour's drive from Ullapool. I stopped here to plod over boggy ground to the edge of Loch na Gainmhich – a harmless-looking body of water surrounded by honey-hued Munros. It was only when I drove on a few minutes more, parked alongside a handful of cars and followed their owners through a narrow gorge, that I understood the full force of this 98-foot-high waterfall. Invisible from the road, it was hard to believe that these veil-like cascades – which drape their way over dark, jagged rocks – were fed by the serene loch I'd just walked beside. I rounded off the day by counting the islands at Badcall Bay and stretching my legs along Scourie Beach, the chatter of cold water swimmers following me as I made my way across the expanse of rock and sand.

The sheer number of stops along the NC500 route can be daunting and some wonders will inevitably be missed, but do make a point of pausing at Smoo Cave, where an underground waterfall blasts you with spray. You should also drink in the view from surfer-revered Dunnet Bay, which is backdropped by the pastel outlines of the Orkney Islands – outposts that seemed so distant when I read about them while plotting my drive in London, but were now only a boat ride away.

Caithness, one of Scotland's most remote counties, was so rugged and wild that driving through it on my fifth day felt almost dreamlike. I ventured close to the clifftops at Sinclair Girnigoe and the Castle of Old Wick, fortified stone ruins that prove castle living wasn't always a comfortable affair; walked among the foundations of

(overleaf) Ardvreck, a skeletal island castle dating from the 15th century

long-gone crofts at the abandoned, gale-lashed Badbea Clearance Village; and braved the Whaligoe Steps – a hand-hewn staircase leading down to an abandoned natural harbour. Descending gingerly in the wind, overtaken with ease by hardy dog walkers, I kept mistaking the crash of waves for rockfall, so it was strange to find the tiny, protected cove still and calm. I sat here for a while admiring the layers and curves in the cliffs, the ripple-like patterns created by 400 million years of maritime and terrestrial deposits left behind by changing sea levels and then pushed around by the rise and fall of moving mountains.

It was an artist who explained the terrain to me. Jenny Mackenzie Ross runs North Coast Pottery and is fascinated by the similarities between her ceramics practice and the processes of the earth. For her, Caithness's sedimentary rock is structurally similar to clay – though the latter is set by her wood-fired kiln, rather than millions of years of pressure.

Jenny is a warden on the John o'Groats Trail, a route founded by American rambler Jay Wilson. Having grown up with the Appalachian Trail in Virginia, Jay came to Scotland keen to walk along the east coast from Inverness to John o'Groats (often said to be the most northerly point on the mainland, despite this title technically belonging to the lighthouse-topped Dunnet Head) but was shocked to find that no such path existed. So, Jay moved to Scotland to create it, aware that rather than extensive funding and infrastructure, all he needed were volunteers like Jenny to guide him over the stretches of coast they knew best.

The NC500 traditionally starts and ends in Inverness, but I wasn't quite ready for my adventure to finish, so I continued to the beaches and distilleries of the sunny Moray Coast – a natural extension of the route. There are ruins aplenty (like the field-framed Duffus Castle and soaring Elgin Cathedral), but it's the whisky that demands your time. Barley thrives here, thanks to the warm microclimate and pristine water supply, and many glens harbour distilleries (incidentally, these glens also doubled as hiding spots centuries ago when high tariffs meant production wasn't always entirely legal). I recommend Glen Grant, with its stunning Victorian gardens, and Glen Moray which, since the early 1900s, has been experimenting with ageing their spirit in different casks. Whisky stored in sherry casks, for example, tastes of Christmas spices, while port barrels add a hint of berries.

On my final morning, while hunting for sea glass along Hopeman Beach, I looked across the bay to the distant dragon's back of Munros, the serrated silhouette bleeding into the amassing cloud. I'd been driving through that stretch of Caithness a few days earlier, but its majesty and scale already felt like it belonged to another faraway world.

Weeks later, home in London with winter setting in, the drive seemed even more surreal. But as I thought back to my time on the road, it was the little moments that stood out: a stone cottage by a loch, an expanse of white sand, a pile of lobster pots lining a quiet harbour. Everything on this route feels deserving of your time, every detail worth drinking in, so it's little wonder that when following the NC500 you get nowhere fast.

(left) The path to Rhue Lighthouse
(overleaf) Balnakeil Beach; The view above Wailing Widow Falls

DIRECTORY

The NC500 begins and ends in Inverness, and a few unmissable stops include Rogie Falls,
Highland Stonewear, Achmelvich Beach, Ardvreck Castle, Wailing Widow Falls, Smoo Cave,
Dunnet Bay, the Orkey Islands, Castle Sinclair Grinigoe and the Whaligoe Steps.

STAY

Kip Hideaways: Ecotone Cabins

Perched among the trees above Loch Broom, these two striking contemporary cabins were built by owner and craftsman Sam Planterose using timber milled from the surrounding forest (he also built most of the furniture in his on-site workshop). Sustainability is at the heart of the project. Sam's ecologist parents bought these 32 acres three decades ago when it was unmanaged and overgrown with rhododendron, spruce and commercial conifers. The family have now replaced these non-native species with deciduous trees, bringing back the diversity and wildlife of a natural Scottish woodland. All proceeds from stays go back into the forest management programme and the outdoor children's nursery run by Sam's sister.

kiphideaways.com/hideaways/forest-cabins-ullapool
Leckmelm Wood, Ullapool, Ross-Shire IV23 2RH GB

Lundies House

Known for its stellar restaurant and immaculate design, this boutique hotel by the Kyle of Tongue comprises four bedrooms in the original manse (which feature wooden floors and marble fireplaces), three bedrooms arranged around the birch-dotted courtyard and a self-contained apartment. Lundies House is part of Wildland, an organisation working to restore and sustainably manage a range of Highland estates.

lundies.scot
Tongue, Lairg IV27 4XF

Links House at Royal Dornoch

With a covetable position beside Royal Dornoch Golf Club (regularly crowned one of the world's best), the 15-bedroom Links House is an homage to old-world Highlands luxury. Its lavish bedrooms are named for renowned local fishing rivers, and filled with antiques, textiles from Johnstons of Elgin (known for their wool since 1797) and paintings that capture some of the landscapes spotted along the NC500.

linkshousedornoch.com
Golf Rd, Dornoch IV25 3LW

Kip Hideaways: Callie Bothy

Built from Scottish larch and insulated by sheep's wool, the hand-crafted, two-person Nature Cabin – enveloped by forest and crowned with an outdoor, wood-fired hot tub – is as inviting as they come. Reached via a single-track road and television free, it's astounding how fast you find yourself slowing down here. Wake with the light and take the time to admire the stars from the wrap-around deck.

kiphideaways.com/hideaways/the-nature-cabin-moray
Lower Calliemuckie, Pluscarden, Elgin, Moray, IV30 8TZ

EAT

The Dipping Lugger

An intimate 18-seat restaurant in a restored 18th-century manse with multi-course lunch and dinner tasting menus that more than justify an Ullapool pilgrimage.

thedippinglugger.co.uk
4 W Shore St, Ullapool IV26 2UR

Lochinver Larder

Pick up an exceptional pie from this Highlands institution that's been fuelling hikers and drivers since 1986. The venison and cranberry and the chestnut, mushroom and red wine varieties are both personal favourites.

lochinverlarder.com
Main St, Lochinver, Lairg IV27 4JY

Kylesku Hotel

Only a short drive from Wailing Widow Falls, and with a history that reaches back to the 17th-century, the Kylesku Hotel's restaurant celebrates exceptional local seafood, with mussels and lobsters caught in the loch the property overlooks.

kyleskuhotel.co.uk
Kylesku, Sutherland, Lairg IV27 4HW

Olive

A community-focused coffee shop a stone's throw from Thurso's surfer-beloved beach that's making waves on the brunch front.

instagram.com/olivethurso
1-3 Brabster St, Thurso KW14 7AP

MARA

Part of Links House at Royal Dornoch, MARA (named for 'sea' in Scots Gaelic) combines contemporary decor with an innovative seafood-heavy regional menu. Most of the seafood hails from Ullapool (my oysters and hand-dived scallops were fished off Shetland) and almost everything else is sourced from within a 35-mile radius.

linkshousedornoch.com/dine/mara
Golf Rd, Dornoch IV25 3LW

Bootleggers

Found along Hopeman's West Beach on the Moray Coast, this restaurant (created from a collection of shipping containers) serves phenomenal seafood – but don't leave without trying the grilled cauliflower, too.

bootleggersbarandgrill.co.uk
Harbour St, Hopeman, Elgin IV30 5RU

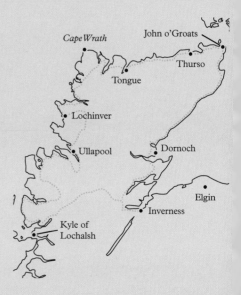

Kip Hideaways: Ecotone Cabin

MARA

Links House at Royal Dornoch

The Dipping Lugger

Kip Hideaways: Ecotone Cabin

Lundies House

Kip Hideaways: Callie Bothy

Bootleggers

Olive

For Isla and Ari, I hope you always find
beauty and wonder in the world around you.

Thank you to Angela Schaffer for always being my first reader, Sarah Kelleher for sharing her thoughts on some of England's ancient marvels, Daisy Wingate-Saul for giving me back my love of photography and Marina Pliatsikas for her brilliant advice and eye. To everyone who has come on a trip, accepted a commission, shared an idea, been generous with their talent or brought a copy of Lodestars, I cannot thank you enough.

Versions of some of these essays initially appeared in *Lodestars Anthology*.

Slow Travel Britain
First edition

Published in 2024 by Hoxton Mini Press, London
Copyright © Hoxton Mini Press 2024. All rights reserved.

Text by Liz Schaffer
Editing by Florence Ward
Design and production by Richard Mason
Proofreading by Zoë Jellicoe

Please note: we recommend checking the websites listed for each directory entry before you visit for the latest information on price, opening times and pre-booking requirements.

ISBN: 978-1-914314-63-6

Printed and bound by PNB Print, Latvia

Hoxton Mini Press is an environmentally conscious publisher, committed to offsetting our carbon footprint. This book is 100 per cent carbon compensated, with offset purchased from Stand For Trees.

Every time you order from our website, we plant a tree: www.hoxtonminipress.com